they taught themselves

they taught themselves

American Primitive Painters of the 20th Century

by Sidney Janis

Foreword by Alfred H. Barr, Jr.
Director, The Museum of Modern Art

KENNIKAT PRESS, INC./PORT WASHINGTON, N. Y.

CONTENTS

PREFACE AND ACKNOWLEDGMENT

FOREWORD BY ALFRED H. BARR, JR.

I. THEY TAUGHT THEMSELVES   3

II. MORRIS HIRSHFIELD, *Cloak and Suit Manufacturer*, 1872–   14

III. WILLIAM DORIANI, *Opera Singer*, 1891–   40

IV. PATRICK J. SULLIVAN, *House Painter*, 1894–   53

V. JOHN KANE, *House Painter*, 1860–1934   76

VI. HENRY CHURCH, *Blacksmith*, 1836–1908   99

VII. JOSEPH PICKETT, *Storekeeper*, 1848–1918   110

VIII. GREGORIO VALDES, *Sign Painter*, 1879–1939   117

IX. ANNA MARY ROBERTSON MOSES, *Farm Wife*, 1860–   128

X. ISREAL LITWAK, *Cabinet Maker*, 1868–   138

XI. PATSY SANTO, *Decorator and House Painter*, 1893–   144

XII. MAX REYHER, *Entomologist and Optician*, 1862–   150

XIII. BERNARD FROUCHTBEN, *Cabinet Maker*, 1872–   154

XIV. CHARLES HUTSON, *Educator and Naturalist*, 1840–1935   160

XV. WILLIAM SAMET, *Inmate, Dannemora Prison*, 1908–   166

XVI. LAWRENCE LEBDUSKA, *Stained-Glass Worker*, 1894–   170

XVII. ELLA SOUTHWORTH, *Housewife*, 1872–   174

XVIII. HAZEL KNAPP, *Former Invalid*, 1908–   178

XIX. RENAULT TOURNEUR, *Prospector*, 1851–   182

XX. HORACE PIPPIN, *Disabled War Veteran (Negro)*, 1888–   187

XXI. GEORGE AULONT, *Jack-of-all-Trades*, 1888–   192

XXII. EMILE BRANCHARD, *Truck Driver*, 1881–1938   196

XXIII. JOSEPHINE JOY, *Housewife*, 1869–   201

XXIV. SAMUEL KOCH, *Milliner*, 1887–   204

XXV. FLORA LEWIS, *Housewife (Negro)*, 1903–   208

XXVI. JESSIE PREDMORE, *Housewife*, 1896–   213

XXVII. GEORGE E. LOTHROP, *Inventor, ?–1929?*   217

XXVIII. CHARLES M. JOHNSON, *Photo-engraver, 1862–*   221

XXIX. PA HUNT, *Sportsman, 1870–1934*   224

XXX. WILLIAM S. MULHOLLAND, *Clergyman, 1870–1936*   227

XXXI. CLEO CRAWFORD, *Laborer (Negro), 1892–1939*   232

XXXII. CONCLUSION   236

PLATES

MORRIS HIRSHFIELD and his painting *Home with Fountains* 14

Beach Girl 21

Angora Cat 27

Lion (*Photo: The Brooklyn Museum*) 29

"Model" for *Lion* 29

Tiger 31

Girl in the Mirror 35

Nude at the Window 39

WILLIAM DORIANI with *Lincoln and Roosevelt* 40

WILLIAM DORIANI *Toe Dancer* 45

Flag Day 46

Rehearsal 49

Theatre 51

PATRICK J. SULLIVAN in his painting corner 53

PATRICK J. SULLIVAN *Man's Procrastinating Pastime* 63

An Historical Event 67

The Fourth Dimension 71

Haunts in the Totalitarian Woods 75

JOHN KANE in his milieu, 1929 76

JOHN KANE Photograph of the actual scene 86
(*Photo: Newman-Schmidt, Pittsburgh*)

From My Studio Window 87

Touching Up 91

Photograph of the actual scene 94
(*Photo: Newman-Schmidt, Pittsburgh*)

Industry's Increase 95

My Grandson 97

HENRY CHURCH, The death notice as it appeared in the *Cleveland Plain Dealer* 99

HENRY CHURCH   *The Rape of the Indian Tribes by the*
                                            White Man. (Rock Carving)   101
                                          Self-Portrait (Photo: Sam Rosenberg)   105
                                          The Monkey Picture (Photo: Sam Rosenberg) 109
JOSEPH PICKETT, Decoration on the facade of his grocery store on
  Mechanic St., New Hope   110
                                          Manchester Valley   115
GREGORIO VALDES, Key West   (Photo: Rudolph Burckhardt)   117
GREGORIO VALDES   Photograph from which the painting
                                            was made (Photo: Rudolph Burckhardt)   122
                                          Paris Scene   123
                                          Cuban Landscape   125
                                          Southernmost House in U. S., Key
                                            West, Florida.   127
ANNA MARY ROBERTSON MOSES in her "studio"   (Photo: Robert C. McCain)   128
ANNA MARY ROBERTSON MOSES *Home*   133
                                          Sugaring Off   135
                                          The Cambridge Valley   137
ISREAL LITWAK coloring *Triboro Bridge*   138
ISREAL LITWAK   *Fifth Avenue*   143
PATSY SANTO in his garden   144
PATSY SANTO   *Hospital Hill*   145
                                          Winter Evening   149
MAX REYHER and his painting, *Wailing Wall*   150
MAX REYHER   *Nirwana*   153
BERNARD FROUCHTBEN at work on *My Ideal*   154
BERNARD FROUCHTBEN   *Lonely Man on a Lonely Road*   159
CHARLES HUTSON on his 94th birthday   160
CHARLES HUTSON   *Carnival in Royal Street*   165
WILLIAM SAMET, Detail of 1940 version, *Cell Interior: Artist at Easel* 168
WILLIAM SAMET   *Cell Interior: Artist at Easel*   169
LAWRENCE LEBDUSKA and *Circus Horses*   170
LAWRENCE LEBDUSKA   *The Flood*   173

ELLA SOUTHWORTH and her paintings against a *"Belgian Panel"*   174

ELLA SOUTHWORTH   *Golden Thoughts*   177

HAZEL KNAPP and her Mother (*Photo: Marshall Brooks*)   178

HAZEL KNAPP   *Guardians of the Valley*   181

RENAULT TOURNEUR   *The Siwanoy Night Patrol*   185

HORACE PIPPIN painting *Woman of Samaria*   186

HORACE PIPPIN   *The End of the War: Starting Home*   191

GEORGE AULONT and *The Arrival of the "New Order" in Crete*   192

GEORGE AULONT   *On Mt. Smolika*   195

EMILE BRANCHARD about 1923 (*Photo: Wide World*)   196

EMILE BRANCHARD   *Farm in Winter*   199

JOSEPHINE JOY working on *Mission Valley Farm*   200

JOSEPHINE JOY   *Dream Garden*   203

SAMUEL KOCH at work on *Coney Island*   204

SAMUEL KOCH   *Union Square*   207

FLORA LEWIS and *Christ and the Woman at the Well*   208

FLORA LEWIS   *Farm Life*   211

JESSIE PREDMORE finishing *Traders*   213

JESSIE PREDMORE   *She's Gone*   215

GEORGE E. LOTHROP, Reverse side of the painting, *The Revelers!*   216

GEORGE E. LOTHROP   *The Revelers!*   219

CHARLES M. JOHNSON and *Roosevelt Speaking*   220

CHARLES M. JOHNSON   *Oslo Winter*   223

PA HUNT, "The borrowed palette is only pose."   224

PA HUNT   *Way Up Along: Provincetown*   225

WILLIAM S. MULHOLLAND in Rupert, Vt.   227

WILLIAM S. MULHOLLAND   *Maple Sugar Making in Vermont*   231

CLEO CRAWFORD and his wife   232

CLEO CRAWFORD   *Christmas*   235

TO H. J.
better known as Hansi

PREFACE AND ACKNOWLEDGMENT

THIS BOOK is a catalogue of experiences, a catalogue of the lives of thirty human beings, of fifty-four paintings. Its reasons for being are to focus attention upon a selection of noteworthy self-taught talents in contemporary American painting, to discuss their works, to record salient experiences on the part of the artists in creating these works.

Its aim is to bring a consciousness to the general art public of the validity of this expression, and also to stimulate those not ordinarily interested in art to find a doorway to this fascinating world.

The primary concern of the book is to establish a record of the high level of achievement sustained by these artists. This is done through a selection of vital and provocative works, among them several that may possess the essentials of timeless art.

Here are stories of how many of the painters were found, of the thrills and experiences of discovery, and episodes revealing the phenomenon of the creative impulse as it grows and thrives in obscurity.

The book is a culmination of an interest of long standing, during which the author found and introduced to the public artists like Sullivan, Doriani and Hirshfield. In idea, it is an extension of an exhibition arranged by the author and sponsored by the Advisory Committee of the Museum of Modern Art in 1939. On this occasion sixteen new talents were introduced and already several of these have had recognition in one-man and in group shows. Among them are Anna (Mother) Moses, Patsy Santo and others.

The sources of biographical information used here, unless otherwise indicated, are the painters themselves, who have given significant material in great detail to the author. Having visited most of these painters over a period of years, the author has had an opportunity to see them work, and has listened to their problems in painting and in their lives. Furthermore, a voluminous correspondence has taken place betwen the author and most of these artists, and there are quotations in the book from this invaluable source —the artists' own words.

Many individuals have made isolated discoveries of talents. The whole meaning of the lives of painters found by them has had so strong an appeal to these individuals, that they have become thoroughly absorbed, and devote much of their energies to this interest. The painter becomes a focus in their lives. In chapters that follow, several of the individuals who made such discoveries will chronicle their experiences with the artists concerned.

The author is cognizant of the existence of scores of aspects but briefly touched upon in the text, so rich, diverse and extensive is the field. A few of these may be summed up as: Psychological Aspects of the Art of the Self-taught; Creative Impulse and the Creative Process; Influence of Social and Geographical Environment on Art; Influence of Vocational Background on the Art of the Self-taught; Logic of the Self-taught Artist; Economics and the Self-taught Artist; Basic Traits and Differences between the Work of Contemporary Primitives and Cave Drawings, Archaic and Primitive Art; Popular Taste and *Popular Art*.

For the past twenty years, the author has been deeply interested in and has made a study of the art of all time, and especially that of the 20th century. The first chapter contains a number of conclusions based on his findings in this extensive research, as applied to the work of the self-taught here and abroad. These conclusions to one who reads only the first chapter may appear arbitrary and unsupported by evidence. However, in the biographies of the painters and the analyses of their paintings, evidence will be found that will serve as documentation for all of these conclusions. In the selection of the 30 artists represented in this book, the work of more than 500 self-taught painters in America was examined.

All of the paintings reproduced are discussed in detail, and in these analyses the author has tried to establish a direct and immediate contact between the reader and the pictures. He has refrained from subjective criticism and obscure generalizations and has attempted instead to discuss in simple terms the specific qualities that give each painting its individual character.

Since the essential aim was to develop a continuity best suited to the nature of the material, the painters and the reproductions of their work do not necessarily appear in the order of their importance.

All those who have graciously helped in the assembling of the material, especially Mr. Sam Rosenberg, who has contributed a colorful biography of Church, are mentioned in the text, and to them a word of thanks for their cooperation. I wish also to thank those who kindly allowed reproduction of pictures from their collections, those who loaned photographs of paintings for use in the book, those who consented to the use of quotations from various publications, to all of whom credit has been given in the text; and the magazine *Decision* for kind permission to reprint several chapters of the book which appeared in the July, 1941, issue. I am grateful to Mr. Lawrence H. Lipskin, who patiently played the role of the public while the book was in progress, and made many helpful suggestions. I want to thank Mr. Alfred H. Barr, Jr., for his sustained interest and support of the work I have been doing in this field, and Mr. André Breton for his sensitive appreciation and understanding. Above all, I am indebted to my wife, Harriet Janis, for the constant faith and creative help which have been so instrumental in making this book a fact.

FOREWORD

EACH generation creates art. It also discovers art. It discovers art both of the more remote past and of the very recent past which we call the present.

Discovery is always followed by evaluation, tentative or confident, original or conventional, sensitive or obtuse. As a result, some discoveries remain in the plane of history and archaeology; others are added to the vast and mutable body of art which we, the living, find psychologically or esthetically valuable.

This book records a voyage of exploration and discovery up a tributary of one of the main streams of modern taste, the "primitive."

Primitive is a term which has been stretched to include a great variety of art from paleolithic sculpture to Alaskan totem poles, and from Italian "primitives" of the 13th century to the modern "primitives," the "popular" or "self-taught" painters, which are the subject of this study. All this immense range of art has one extraordinary thing in common: it has been discovered esthetically and revalued within the past hundred years and mostly in the last fifty.

In fact it was just about fifty years ago that the greatest modern primitive, Henri Rousseau of France, was first given some appreciative recognition. Rousseau was not entirely self-taught but his psychological and pictorial innocence, his naive realism and fantasy and his independence of tradition have made him the archetype of all painters of his kind. It is this last characteristic, independence of school or tradition which distinguishes these painters psychologically and genetically from all other kinds of primitives, even from children who work in schools and often imitate each other. Their independence and isolation is revealed not only in their art but in their biographies so interestingly presented in this book.

Perhaps it is imprudent to try to evaluate the importance of the self-taught artists in comparison with other schools or kinds of living artists. Some of the painters in this book seem to me so obviously superior to others that I wish Mr. Janis had not been quite so generously inclusive. But it is by its finest artists that a school or movement should be judged and I for one think that, just as Rousseau now seems one of the foremost French painters of his generation, certain of our self-taught painters can hold their own in the company of their best professionally trained compatriots. Among 20th century American paintings I do not know a finer landscape than Joseph Pickett's *Manchester Valley*, a more unforgettable animal picture than Hirshfield's *Tiger*, a more original metaphysical composition than Sullivan's *Fourth Dimension*, or a more moving portrait than John Kane's painting of himself.

It is significant that artists were among Rousseau's first admirers, Gauguin, Toulouse-Lautrec, Degas in the '90's and, later, Picasso, Leger, Brancusi, Max Weber and the critics Apollinaire and Uhde. In this country, too, certain painters, Walt Kuhn, Charles Sheeler, Andrew Dasburg, for instance, were among the first to praise the work of living self-taught artists, and to these pioneer explorers may be added the museum workers Holger Cahill and Dorothy Miller and the critic-dealers J. B. Neumann and Stephan Bourgeois, though none of these has produced a book on the subject comparable in scale and thoroughness to this work by Sidney Janis.

Sidney Janis is a collector and *amateur* as well as an explorer. I have followed with interest the development of his taste and of his collection from an early interest in expressionism through a remarkably discriminating eclecticism which lead him to acquire excellent works by Picasso, Klee, Dali and a famous masterpiece by Henri Rousseau. It was perhaps the long and intimate study of his Rousseau which inspired him to concentrate so enthusiastically upon the art of the self-taught American artist.

Though he has had much intense, direct experience of pictures he is not an academically trained art historian nor a professional critic and writer. There is indeed something about the method and spirit of this book which seems peculiarly in harmony with its self-taught subjects—and by this I mean to compliment and commend the author. For Sidney Janis has brought to his work a painstaking conscientiousness, a warm enthusiasm, a tireless zeal which makes me think at times of the artists whose paintings he so admires.

ALFRED H. BARR, JR.

they taught themselves

CHAPTER ONE

THEY TAUGHT THEMSELVES

ABRAHAM LINCOLN, the self-made man of history, is the idol of American self-taught artists of today. The drama of the figure whose life was so touching and tragic and human, whose achievements were so profound, inevitably attracts them. The fact that almost every self-taught American painter I have encountered has painted a portrait of Abraham Lincoln may well be regarded as an interesting symbol of their activity. There is much in the significance of the life of Lincoln with which they can identify themselves. His obscure beginnings, his silent struggles with knowledge and his open conflicts with life are their own. They wish for themselves the greatness that was his, and his martyrdom draws them close.

Artists among the People

This vital group of painters living in America has had little encouragement or recognition. They come from all walks of life. Some are craftsmen—cabinet-makers, house-painters, decorators, blacksmiths—but they may also be tradesmen, housewives, laborers. All of them are motivated by an inner drive to paint, and this they do in their spare time. On the Continent they have been affectionately called *Sunday Painters*.

3

These folk are not a phenomenon of our time. There have always been such artists among the people. Invariably they work quietly, away from any contact with Art. The world of art is desirable but as remote as a dream. Although they may contribute to it, they rarely become a part of it.

The greatest and most famous of them all, Douanier Rousseau, died in Paris in 1910. The public imagination has been greatly stimulated by the posthumous recognition of Rousseau, who was for the most part ridiculed except by a few perceiving artists and poets who admired him only near the end of his life. Understanding of the real character of this great artist's work, and subsequent acceptance of it by the world at large, have awakened interest in self-taught expression.

Perhaps this has resulted in a quickened awareness of the inherent qualities of our own self-taught artists, both contemporary and of the past.

Devotees of Americana constitute a receptive audience for our primitive itinerant painters and anonymous artists of the 18th and early 19th centuries, although the approach of this group is often enough based on historical interest and national sentiment as well as esthetic evaluation. As a matter of fact, it is on that period that most of the interest in American self-taught artists is centered, for we find that primitives of the late 19th century and today do not share this recognition.

"Decline" in the Art of the People

It would appear from the studies already made in this field, that the tradition of art of the people, which flourished so profusely in America, reached an apotheosis in the second quarter of the 19th century and declined with the advent of a new era of science and industry. As the camera gained favor, the itinerant portrait painter, who had done the finest of this early self-taught work, was gradually eliminated from the scene. When the family album appeared on the table, ancestor paintings began to find their way to the attic, from the obscurity of which they were not to emerge until the second quarter of the 20th century. The spaces left on the walls as these primitives came down, were covered with lithographs and chromos, and the first period of Currier & Ives' great popular appeal had got under way.

Hand-craftsmen, whose skills led them naturally into esthetic expression,

4

were now separated from their crafts by the machine, and these hand-skills went into disuse.

The tremendously increased speed of travel by land and by sea brought a resurgence of foreign influences in art, and the consumer interest now became divided between chromos and lithographs on the one hand, and a vast amount of derivative and banal art on the other, which at present reposes in the basements of so many of our museums.

All of this new activity, together with the upheaval caused by the Civil War and the period of reconstruction which followed it, seems to indicate that there had been a decline in self-taught expression, but the decline may actually have been one in appreciation rather than creation.

If for the most part the early American painters remained anonymous, it is probably because their work was not properly evaluated as art in their day, but was considered mainly as mere portraiture, commissioned for sentimental reasons. As already indicated, rediscovery of these early works today involves two facets of appreciation: one, their acceptance after a safe margin of time has elapsed; and the other, one of those unpredictable turns in esthetic appreciation which brings a new awareness.

It is therefore reasonable to assume that there may have been no decline at all, for the self-taught artist is a perennial worker, paying his tribute quietly to those sources deep within human nature from which the creative impulse springs. He thrives in spite of external conditions. He does not lean on an established painting tradition. He is spiritually independent.

Certainly the fact remains that today, in the midst of an age of highly specialized mechanization and industrialization, when it might be expected that this expression would be at low ebb, there are scores of self-taught painters of outstanding merit working among the people. They are worthy successors to our 18th and 19th century anonymous portraitists, and they work with an originality more varied, incorporating a much wider latitude of expression.

If a comprehensive research and appraisal of the field was not made and published in times past, the reasons for it may be understood. But there is no valid reason why such an important task should not be fully organized and carried on in connection with our contemporary self-taught artists.

5

Efforts to Bring Works to Light

Any appreciative activity in this field has until recently operated only through isolated efforts of individuals, organizations, and galleries. People with a generally developed appreciation and with contact with European works of this nature responded to men like John Kane and Joseph Pickett, the first of these 20th century American painters to receive recognition. A few New York galleries exhibited the works of self-taught artists. These artists were also seen by chance at such general showings as the exhibits of the Society of Independent Artists, the Washington Square Outdoor Art Mart, the Southern Vermont Artists' Association at Manchester, where men like Branchard, Sullivan, Doriani and Mulholland were found.

The first coordinated effort in this country to show them as a homogeneous group was in 1938, in the *Masters of Popular Painting* exhibit at the Museum of Modern Art. Here both European and American *popular masters* were shown, and the thirteen Americans included were for the most part already known.

The Unknown

In 1939 at an exhibition called *Contemporary Unknown American Painters* sponsored by the Advisory Committee of the Museum of Modern Art and shown in the Members' Rooms of that museum, sixteen new self-taught talents were introduced. My object in assembling the exhibition was to stimulate interest in unknowns, among whom might be artists of distinction whose merits were still to be properly evaluated. In this way, it was hoped, the inevitable time-lag between the creation of works of art and their appreciation might be shortened. For the living non-professional finds a public little prepared to encourage him since it has had only a limited opportunity to orient itself to his work, and he has for the most part yet to find his audience.

Potential Audience for the Work of the Self-Taught

There is ample reason why lovers of art should be drawn to his work, but the audience need not be restricted to the world of art, for the self-taught artist expresses himself with a humility and an easily comprehended human

6

quality that may be shared by everyone. The layman may also be attracted, for example, by the theme, by visual ideas that move close to his own experience, or by the human-interest aspect of the self-taught; he may be tempted to seek out such an artist, or perhaps even to paint. For the psychologist there is rich material in this field, because the expression, unhampered by a complex painting culture, is so direct and close to the surface that the functioning of psychological processes in general may be readily examined. For the same reason he may find a clearer path to the phenomenon of the creative process itself. And to those interested in art as, first and foremost, an authentic esthetic experience, there is also the adventure and pleasure of making vital discoveries.

By Way of Evaluation

The art of all time, and particularly the profound development in international painting which centered in Paris during the 20th century, have demonstrated the wisdom of determining the validity of any expression on the basis of its own terms, not losing sight of the fact that there are constants in all art. This is true, whether the expression be one of a given culture or sub-culture, such as Assyrian, Etruscan, Coptic or Gothic, or of individuals within a culture, as for example, Cezanne, Picasso, Duchamp and Klee, who are close to each other in the same painting stream. It is essential that this attitude be brought to contemporary self-taught art, especially since each artist's work may be regarded as unique and must, in the main, be evaluated individually.

The Innocents

Whatever the reasons may be, there are people in the world who always retain an untouched quality, a spiritual innocence, regardless of their experiences in life. Somewhere within them is an impregnable quality carried over from childhood, which experience does not assail. It is a spontaneous innate uncommon sense which remains inviolate in the face of outwardly imposed tensions and restraints. When these individuals paint, they rarely learn from a developed painting culture because it is far removed from their perception, and being removed, cannot touch them. Each creates in his own world.

7

Often a surprising enterprise and courage are born of their very innocence. Not realizing the pitfalls, they are unafraid.

In the work of the most interesting of these artists, through sureness of intuition, a harmony is achieved between emotion and idea, and the medium through which they are expressed. Unlike either the work of the untutored child, which develops with his years, or that of the studied artist, which evolves in comprehension and craft, the painting of the self-taught artist most frequently comes to virtual fruition with the making of his first picture.

Why They Paint

Every child draws, as witness the sidewalks of New York, for drawing is a form of creative expression latent in every human being. Some people develop this by study and become professional artists. Or they may push it aside so that it remains hidden until specific drives bring it to the surface again. In this category are the self-taught artists. Before actually painting, they go through a series of rudimentary unconsummated painting gestures which help to mature them. Often these cursory gestures are tied up with their crafts, as in the case of house-painters, sign-painters, furniture-finishers, cabinet-makers, decorators, needlecraft workers, who are naturally led into painting as an extension of already developed motor activity. It is interesting to note that many of the self-taught painters have such backgrounds, and frequently many aspects of their work spring directly from occupational activities. But others who do not, still have what may be called a "craft sense" about their tasks; conscientious, ingenious, deft, they obtain an esthetic gratification in the same way as do craftsmen in the execution of their crafts.

Reasons for their painting may also be found in their environment, which plays its part. In communities where they are surrounded by profuse art activity, social condemnation is eliminated. They then paint either because others do or because they feel challenged by the work of others. In any event they leap their first hurdle.

Some specific drives to paint are very much the same as those of the professional artist. Aided and abetted by coordination between visual experience

8

and manual dexterity, they may paint because they have a message to impart; because they have been painting pictures in their minds for years and are finally impelled to carry this into overt action; because they have psychological situations to resolve through sublimation or because frustration of a given talent must provide another outlet.

Critical Innocence and the Self-Taught Artist

Unevenness in the work of the self-taught painter is greater than in the work of the studied artist. Moreover his fine pictures and his poor ones are apt to be equally acceptable to him. This critical innocence is responsible for his going to extremes in both directions. It is for this reason that those of his pictures which "come off" reach far into the field of distinction, compensating generously for the canvases that fail. With the more gifted painter the percentage of good painting is consistently high, ample proof, if proof be needed, that his achievements are not the result of accident.

Sometimes self-taught artists ardently desire to paint realistically, as Rousseau did when he admired Bouguereau and yearned to paint like him. It is apparent from what they say about their work that they believe they are faithfully recording reality. However, even cursory examination shows that a great disparity exists between what they believe and what they actually have accomplished. Although convinced that they have made a photographic reproduction of the world of reality, they have actually transmuted it into a new, pictorial reality. For whether painting reality, fantasy, allegory, or any of the endless types of art upon which a self-taught artist focuses, he functions with the utmost freedom. Forever finding himself in fresh and untried fields, he must forever invent, create and discover.

Of course he does not always succeed. On the contrary much self-taught art is crude and sentimental in the extreme. Colored postcards, calendars, chromos, often make up the artist's environment, and his work may be only too frequently little more than imitative. But one encounters occasionally an artist able to borrow from even these dubious sources and elevate his material by inventive and creative handling.

9

Paradox in Paint

Paradoxically, although the self-taught artist does not make a selection from the complex and developed painting tradition of today, he often independently achieves isolated results that parallel those of cultivated expressions. In his own way, he may quite unwittingly arrive at such results in the process of converting his concept into painting terms.

For instance, knowing nothing of Cubism, he may paint a picture in which a circulating viewpoint is used, or one that is counterpoised like a cubist painting. Knowing nothing of Surrealism, he may create enigmatic surface textures, use literary ideas and fantasies that are closely akin to Surrealism. Knowing nothing of Freud, he may undesignedly employ symbols similar to those Dali uses with specific intent.

With many of the self-taught painters, psychological factors which are tied up with inner conflicts of various kinds are of primary importance. The necessity for working out their psychological problems furnishes one of the mainsprings out of which their pictorial means flow, for through sublimation in paint, they resolve their doubts, their emotions and their beliefs. In men like Hirshfield, Sullivan, Samet, Frouchtben, it is at the root of their need to paint. This may be observed in individual works by these artists reproduced here, and is enlarged upon in the accompanying discussions.

Primitive Character of the Self-Taught

The primitive character in the works of contemporary self-taught painters is essentially unlike that in cave drawings, which are the product of primitive culture with primitive tools. Because of their striving for space ideas and sometimes because of their use of form and color, their work stands closer to the primitive paintings of the 14th century. It also has characteristics of folk-art in its pleasing awkwardness and humble spirit. Still it bears the stamp of its own time. Not only do fashions in clothes, furniture, decorations and the like, used in the paintings, reveal this, but attitudes of mind which inevitably come to these artists from the larger environment as well as from the commonplace experiences of their daily lives.

10

The Primitive in Modern Art

On the other hand, there is a primitive character and a true primitive synthesis in the work of certain very advanced moderns, for they too embody the force and austerity of purpose that accompany any initial struggle with art forms.

However, in these instances, this struggle occurs as a break with a tradition of which there is a highly developed awareness on the part of the artist, whereas with the self-taught painter there is no consciousness at all of a tradition, only of an individual directness of purpose.

For instance, in Leger, the stark quality of early beginnings pertains to the machine rather than to nature, but the elemental quality is still there, and his modern forms do not disguise it. It is perhaps for this very reason that he found in Rousseau a common spirit. Although there is no superficial emulation of Rousseau in his work, Leger is a primitive poet of the machine as Rousseau is of nature.

Picasso had found this spirit in African Negro sculpture as well as in Rousseau, as he has found nuclei in passing through all esthetic experience. He incorporated it, together with a direct primitive power as well as a more dynamic and penetrating interpretation of the archaic, in his work, as a part of its total and very complex expression.

Near-Primitives

There are painters who may be called near-primitive. They are not unaware of painting traditions, but for one reason or another seek to express themselves with naiveté. Their work always has a simulated look because they never can capture the true quality of the primitive.

In Search of a Name

The confusion caused by the various descriptive terms for *self-taught artist* leads one to ponder the problem of a name that will convey without ambiguity his place in the world of art. This problem is somewhat complicated by the fact that there are many categories of contemporary self-taught artists.

We find for example that Doriani paints humorous folk-art; Sullivan,

11

whose work has the feeling of Mantegna, paints philosophical themes, while Hirshfield derives from psychological-instinctive sources. The New England landscapes of Moses, Southworth, Santo, Pa Hunt and Knapp are lyric and pictorial; those of Rev. Mulholland are spiritual in a religious sense. The direct approach, as it exists in child-art, is part of the elemental character of the work of Litwak, Crawford and Hutson. Church, the blacksmith, creates robust and Victorian fantasy, and the fantasy of Reyher springs from themes in poetry and the science of entomology.

These few examples demonstrate that there is a rich variety in the work of our contemporary self-taught artists, and it is important for this reason that a name be selected which is comprehensive enough to cover them all in one expressive category.

A variety of names has been used, none of them adequate. Some appear in this book because their specific gradations of meaning are effective. In the past, those most frequently used have been: *Non-professionals,* which is too general; *Sunday Painters,* affectionate but hardly accurate; *Popular Painters,* which suggests the popularity of song hits and *Painters of the People,* an agreeable name but too inclusive. The term *Folk-artist* implies a person who makes rural or peasant art and directs his efforts to objects made primarily for use. *Instinctives* they are, but they are very much more than this.

Naives, a name which in its purest meaning implies those who are artless, ingenuous, refreshingly innocent, may well apply. But unfortunately through common usage it calls to mind ignorance. Most frequently used is the term *Primitives,* which, although usage gives it a very wide application, is limited for our purpose. It may therefore seem that the combined term *Naive-Primitives* most closely approximates the category under which these artists might be generally grouped. But besides being cumbersome, it still carries undesirable overtones.

The title, *Self-taught Artists,* which is favored by the author, adequately describes them, and is at the same time unassuming. While the definition as it stands might be stretched to include non-primitives, such as those who paint more or less academically, or even schooled artists who have rebelled

12

against their schooling, there are apart from this, no implications to spoil its meaning. The term *autodidactic*, which André Breton suggests, comes even nearer an accurate description. But this is already associated with the sophisticated self-taught among the surrealist painters, who work with full knowledge of the tradition of art. *Naive-Primitive*, then, is probably the most concise term, but *Self-taught*, which audience reaction also favors because of its close tie to everyday life, is used in the text as a more satisfactory one.

MORRIS HIRSHFIELD and his painting, *Home with Fo*

CHAPTER TWO

MORRIS HIRSHFIELD

WHILE ASSEMBLING paintings for the exhibition of *Contemporary Unknown American Painters* at the Museum of Modern Art, I met a picture dealer on the street. He told me he had paintings by a Negro artist whose

14

work he believed would fit into this exhibition. This proved to be the work of Horace Pippin, who had previously been shown at the *Masters of Popular Painting* exhibition and was therefore no longer unknown.

About to leave the gallery, I peeked at a picture whose face was to the wall. What a shock I received! In the center of this rather square canvas, two round eyes, luminously gleaming in the darkness, were returning my stare! It brought to mind the sequence in *Duck Soup* in which Groucho Marx, confronted by an unexpected image in his mirror, was taken aback, only to find the image oddly enough immobile. The image I saw was just as unexpected and the round unflinching eyes continued to stare, impervious to my sudden start. They belonged to a strangely compelling creature which, sitting possessively upon a remarkable couch, immediately took possession of me. This was my introduction to the work of Hirshfield.

The picture was *Angora Cat*. I asked if there were any other paintings by this man, and the dealer, Hudson Walker, turned from the wall two more that stood nearby, remarking that the artist had left them for a few days. He asked what I thought of them. My reply was to borrow two of the three paintings at once for the exhibition, and.a moment later I left with the canvases under my arm.

At the opening of the *Unknowns* exhibition in the Members' Rooms, a short elderly man with reddish blonde hair quietly approached me and said he was Hirshfield. He was happy that his pictures were shown in "such a grand place" and he began at once to tell of his long struggle to achieve the two canvases hung there before us. He had painted three pictures, and these were his first two. He had begun *Beach Girl* two years before and had set it aside to begin *Angora Cat*. From then on he worked intermittently on both of them, finally finishing them together.

As will be seen in the psychological unfolding throughout his work, described in the analyses of his paintings which follow, Hirshfield's difficulties arose from tensions in his home environment from which, as he informed me at this time, he received little encouragement to paint. He has a wife, three grown children, an unmarried daughter to whom he is especially attached, a son, and a married daughter who has two children.

The next picture he wanted to do was a lion, and he had searched for a

15

model at the zoo, the public library, and the American Museum of Natural History, but to no avail. A week later, when we met again, he had found his lion in a toy shop and had begun his drawing. That is was a trite, colored lithograph with a three-quarter front view of a savage lion* was of little moment to Hirshfield. It may have served as a point of departure, but I do not believe it did even that. It was related emotionally to something that he already had in mind. It was a sort of corroboration. Two pictures, *Lion* and *Tiger*, reproduced here, were needed before he could be satisfied that he had obtained what he was looking for in his lion model.

In an effort to get the mane of the lion to resemble hair, Hirshfield first used a fine comb. (It will be remembered that Picasso and Braque obtained textures in Cubist paintings by the same means. Naturally, Hirshfield knows nothing of Cubism.) His idea was to comb the pigment into place, but he did not get the result he wanted. Therefore with a brush he painstakingly worked out the individual strands throughout the mane, building up the pigment for each detail. The textural result fully justifies the tremendous effort spent.

It is Hirshfield's practise to start a picture by making an outline drawing of his main subject. He executes this in full scale on paper and then traces it upon his canvas. From then on, his work in paint begins. His landscapes and skies are painted directly on the canvas without first being drawn.

Unlike Doriani, for instance, whose preliminary drawings are as complete as his paintings, Hirshfield gives no indication in his sketches of what he is able to do with paint. His drawings are commonplace, but when he begins to work in pigment, he elevates his concept with inspired intensity. Vitality and invention, lacking in his drawings, come through in paint. To Hirshfield the reality is the actual brush stroke, the manipulation of paint and of color. The hard pencil is simply a means to an end, but working in pigment is a labor of love. He cherishes his paintings, but destroys his drawings, and has only lately saved a few to show to me.

This feeling for pigment, together with the uninhibited state in which he approaches his work, enables him to find the way to achieve his unusual textures. The sensation produced by these textures is so strong, that it is

* Reproduced bottom of p. 29.

16

difficult to resist the temptation to touch them. When the painting *Tailor-Made Girl* returned from an exhibition, the nose, which is in relief, was blackened by fingermarks.

Let us now read the story of his life so that later we may examine the effect of his experiences upon his work.

MY LIFE BIOGRAPHY
by
MORRIS HIRSHFIELD

Born in 1872 in a small town of about 1000 inhabitants in Russia-Poland near German border. Mother was German born; father a native of Russia-Poland.

It seems that even in my young days I exhibited artistic tendencies—not in painting —but in wood-carving, for at the tender age of 12 I aroused our little town by producing for myself a unique noise-maker to be used in the Jewish *Purim* festivals at the synagogue. On this noise-maker I managed to depict the main event of the *Purim* day by modeling in wood actual miniature figures of the well-known Jewish biblical characters Mordecai, his adopted cousin Esther, Haman and King Xerxes. . . . I painted the features to make the appearance more lifelike and actually clothed them in garments I felt befitted their day.

The furor it created was so great that the Rabbi of that congregation was compelled to go to my father pleading that he hide my work-of-art in order that prayers could be rendered.

Seeing my work so well received and admired, I took courage to go on to even greater efforts. At the age of fourteen I undertook the sculpturing in wood of a piece of work almost six feet high for our local synagogue. It formed the prayer stand in front of the scroll on which the Cantor's prayer-books rested. It consisted of two huge lions holding between them the ten commandments. Below the animals were two prayer books lying flat, and on top of the holy volumes were two birds, one holding in his beak a pear, the other a leaf. Everything was carved in full life-like figures and embossed with a good many more ornamental designs which I do not remember in detail and the whole gilded with gold and other colors of paint. . . .

Unless destroyed by the ravages of recent warfare, it still holds its place of honor in the synagogue for I have been told by kinsfolk recently arrived from my home town that when they left it was still standing. . . .

At the age of eighteen I left Europe and came to America where I found a position as worker in a woman's coat factory. After being in the line several years I became engaged and thus stimulated, went into business with my brother in the manufacturing of woman's coats and suits, the firm being known as Hirshfield Brothers. During this period I married.

I stayed in this line for twelve years. While we were making a very nice line of merchandise we could not call it a financial success, so we sold the business and shortly thereafter entered a new field—the manufacturing of boudoir slippers, where I made

17

a huge success, employing over three hundred people. The E. Z. Walk Mfg. Co., as I called it, soon became the biggest manufacturing plant of its kind in N.Y.C.

During all these years, although busy manufacturing, I never quite stifled my strong urge to produce artistically, to paint or carve—although I never quite actually managed to settle down to work on anything. I did turn out several inventions, however, patented in Washington.

After being at the head of the E. Z. Walk Mfg. Co. for fifteen years and enjoying an enviable rating and a well-known name and doing a business of about a million a year, I was suddenly stricken ill and during my long absence the place was so badly managed that on my return I found it impossible to go on. I retired then from active business.

My first paintings, on which I worked so laboriously and which took me so long to produce, were started in 1937 and were called The *Beach Girl* and *Angora Cat*.

It seems that my mind knew well what I wanted to portray but my hands were unable to produce what my mind demanded. After working five months on one and then the other in 1937 I could not carry them out to my satisfaction and so put them to one side, coming back again to them in 1938, when once again, I worked on them for about five or six months. While they were muchly improved, they still did not satisfy me and so again I put them to one side. It was when I took them up again in 1939 for the third time that I brought them out to my entire satisfaction.

Hirshfield's occupational background has a very important role in his paintings. We find it in his textures, which remind one of various fabrics, and in his sense of design, which comes from pattern-making. His large drawings are really patterns, and sometimes he will even directly cut out a form to serve as a pattern. He did this in his *Home with Fountains*, cutting out of cardboard the contour of a bird which he used in four different positions and colorings. He perforated the wings for the same reason that garment patterns are perforated, so that the perforations might be a working guide. The continuous line which flows through all of Hirshfield's work is an extension of the rhythmic sensation which accompanies the motor action of cutting around the contours of patterns.

He paints in his bedroom, but he does not use an easel. He leans his canvases on the dresser against the mirror and in this position paints with infinite care. When his brushes become stubby, he trims them. His pictures completed, he takes the measurements to his framer, where he carefully selects a frame which he believes suitable. Invariably he chooses a patterned shiny gilt design reminiscent of the affluent days when he "bought beautiful furniture at auction rooms." Judging from his descriptions, they were expensive pieces with lavish marble tops and profuse mother-of-pearl inlay; Oriental tabourets, and gilt chairs. His frames are definitely more restrained, but still belong to this environment. They are a reflection of his taste when it does not pass through the wisdom of his intuition as do the objects in his paintings.

Self-taught artists often communicate with their local museums for advice or recognition, a practise which seems to me to be very intelligent, for it is natural that a museum should be the center of activity for artists in its community. After each picture is framed, Hirshfield takes it to the Brooklyn Museum where his friend, John I. H. Baur, curator, has it photographed. With the exception of his first three pictures, the Museum has a complete photographic record of his work to date.

Hirshfield has definite opinions about art, especially the painting of his contemporaries, finding many of them "too crude for my taste." However, when he first saw the paintings of John Kane, he admired the "good detail work," and of Sullivan he said "this is serious work." At an exhibition of local artists at the Brooklyn Museum in 1940, which included one of his canvases, he took my arm and said he wanted to show me a *real* work. He led me to a portrait of a young girl, and remarked in awe, "I would like to meet this artist and shake his hand. This is real work and I would give anything if I could do it." The only reply I could make was, "I hope you never will." It was a pretty and sentimental picture in the worst manner of the British portraitists of the late 18th century.

Pictorial logic in the paintings of Hirshfield is such an extensive subject that the reader is referred directly to the analyses, where the manner in which it works can best be observed. Various points are made in connection with each picture, and a specific continuity is developed throughout the works touched upon. It may be of interest, however, to mention in passing the logic which guided the making of a few pictures not included here. In *Tailor-Made Girl*, Hirshfield points with pride to the fact that both sides of the tailored suit are exactly alike, "as it should be in a well-made suit of clothes." In his portraits of houses, each house is also bi-symmetrically planned, as if well-made clothes and well-made houses alike must be balanced. This of course does not mean that Hirshfield conceives his work in terms of arid bi-symmetry. On the contrary, we find great compositional variation not only in his individual paintings, but in his whole production as an integrated *oeuvre*.

19

Beach Girl

BEACH GIRL is Hirshfield's first picture. It is painted on an old canvas. Hirshfield seems to have retained as a nucleus a face from the picture that was formerly on the canvas and developed his own remarkable painting around it, gradually obliterating the rest of the painting which was underneath.

He has smoothed out the contour of the face until it is a carefully carved oval, and added green Leonardo-like flesh tones and shadowings to the golden brown modeling that was already there. If he has in any way followed more of the figure that was underneath, this is lost in the complete originality of his own conception.

He has taken possession of any borrowings as a creative artist always does, by incorporating them within his own personality so thoroughly that they become an integral part of his own expression.

Painting Paradox

Unaware of Dada or Surrealism, he has worked in the same way as for example Max Ernst and Salvador Dali. Dali, it will be remembered, collaged the photograph of a head of a lion in his painting, *Accommodations of Desire*, 1929, and Ernst conversely produced the same effect in his book *La Femme 100 Têtes*, where among other things he used an entire figure from an old steel engraving and drew upon it a head of his own making. These knowing artists consciously borrowed images to heighten the surprise evoked by the juxtaposition of common objects in uncommon relationships. They did this not only to create a vital esthetic in their own terms, but also as Marcel Duchamp had previously done, for the purpose of prodding the observer to an alert response to esthetic experience. Unconsciously Hirshfield, by the same relating of the unexpected, has caused the same element of surprise. The strangeness created by the use of this face, so startlingly unlike his own painting in character, is homogeneous with the strange and captivating quality of the picture as a whole. It is highly conceivable to one

20

HIRSHFIELD *Beach Girl.* 1937

who knows the artist that he retained this face because he thought it "so perfect" that he could never approach such perfection.

Feminine Characteristics

Hirshfield has created a girl whom he speaks of as his "dream girl," and she is, in effect, the essence of a total experience with womanhood. She has the hands and feet of a small child, the legs of an adolescent, the face of a grown young woman and the torso of mature womanhood. The background, too, is part of this experience, for it has textures that are membranous, forms that convolute, colors that are aqueous. The figure of the modest and timid girl standing as she does on a sandy stretch of beach between two huge forms would suggest, psychoanalytically, a phallus, and the composition as a whole would conjure up puerperal and coitive contexts.

Although Hirshfield intended to portray no more than a young girl playing on a beach, his intuition proved stronger than his conscious intention. For little did the artist suspect that in recording his "ideal girl," he was depicting a woman who had experienced the natural fullness of a normal life.

The artist dedicated himself to this picture. Deeply felt, it is worked through to the utmost of his creative powers, a fact to which it owes its remarkable intensity. Not a little of this is due to the halo of darkness around the girl's figure, which, picked up in the lavender grey shadings on the sand, and enhanced by the forms that all but envelop her, isolates the girl in an atmosphere of mystery.

The Subject Matter

She stands on a narrow strip of sandy beach washed by slate blue sea waves on either side. Above her white clouds are swirling against a deep blue sky. Because of the general configuration of the waves and their fine grainings, I originally believed them to be large rocks, and I thought the clouds were actually waves breaking across the top of the picture on the beach. One day, however, in looking at the picture with Hirshfield, he asked if I felt there were too many clouds. Not only had I been misled by the configuration and grainings referred to above, but the total intuitive concept had

22

caused me to see solid formations instead of waves, and wavy fluid movements instead of clouds. But especially was I put off by the unorthodox water-line of the horizon, which is curvilinear. For the moment I had forgot that the more important consideration here, pictorial design, had ruled out the natural law that water seeks its own level.

Curvilinear Movements

A straight horizon line for the water would have disrupted the entire composition, which consists of curving lines flowing in and about in myriad changing directions. These movements begin rather quietly and simply in the oval shapes in the pail. The oval is repeated in the face, and the curling lines of the braids follow these contours, the whole being finally crowned by the halo of the hat. The shorts are gently creased down the center, from which carefully fashioned green folds curl and radiate.

The tempo picks up in the white blouse, where a complex variety of curving lines plays. The curves are used here like modeling, to suggest the form concealed beneath. In the water, the movements increase in number and in complexity. This is stepped up in the sand and here they become groping tendrils. The theme comes to a climax across the top of the picture, where variegated undulations of white clouds constantly work in opposition to each other. This ever-changing panorama moves in front of the deep blue of the sky.

Textures

Textures augment the effectiveness of the curvilinear composition. They are conceived with a high degree of originality and invention. They arouse strong visual and tactile responses, even to the degree of inviting the touch. In the landscape the three fundamentals, land, water, sky are transformed from naturalistic into imaginative elements, each of these elements giving several experiences, the least of which are associated with nature.

This phenomenon in imaginative painting of a given object having two or more conceivable associations is not an uncommon one. For example, in the Surrealist frottage *Natural History* by Max Ernst, he rubbed on paper the grainings of wood surfaces as a child rubs in the face of a coin. The gen-

23

eral formation suggested to him a chimerical bird and the large grainings of the wood became its feathers. The finer grainings assumed a completely different character, that of the texture of burlap. Through all this, the rubbings of the grain of the wood still retained their original identity.

In *Beach Girl* the waves are stippled and grained like the pores and ridges on two huge thumbprints, or the surface of Inwood limestone, a rock formation found in New York City. Their pigment strokes give the impression of interminable stitchings on the interlining of clothing, and the all-over effect of texture and color is that of woven salt-and-pepper tweed.

The sand is furrowed by rivulets of water, and the corrugations formed are like the circulatory systems in organic and plant matter, causing the sand to resemble at once a reef of white coral and the inner surface of tripe.

In the clouds, the texture, like the color and delineation, has the quality of fluffy feathers which air currents are driving into individual convoluting channels.

Through Hirshfield's former experience with the making of women's apparel, he has imparted to the fabrics of the girl's garb a special intimacy that comes with the understanding of their substance. The folds in the shorts are as supple as silk. The striated texture in the white blouse brings to mind a kind of terry cloth. He has also given to the landscape the character of various textiles, for the tweed effects in the waves and the patterns in the sand and sky have associations with novel and fleecy materials used in women's wear.

The face, which is very smoothly painted, is encased in a horseshoe wreath of thick brown braids. The brim of the hat is smooth again, and as the color grades from deep violet to light blue, the rim is accentuated by a built-up ridge of white pigment. The heaviest incrustation of paint surrounds the legs of the girl, which are rendered doubly smooth by contrast. How fortunate that the girl floats rather than stands, for her bare feet might otherwise be cut by the sharp coral reef! Hirshfield has placed her in a two-dimensional world, for regardless of the illusion of receding space suggested by the shore lines, the girl, the sand, the water and sky are all on the same vertical picture plane.

24

Angora Cat

ANGORA CAT is a strange mysterious creature. She is at once spell-binding and mirth-provoking. Her deep-set eyes, staring intensely, take immediate possession of the beholder, and they hold him with the suspense of a mystery thriller. But she is such a homey creature, round and fluffy, that the terror is not quite convincing, and the ripples of fear that run up and down the spine eventually turn to laughter. She is an exciting, upsetting creature, whom one cannot help but love.

As indicated in the biography of Hirshfield, this possessive cat was symbolic of a conflict at home, where at this time he received little encouragement to paint. The conflict kept coming between him and his ideal, the desire to paint, which was consummated for the first time in the picture *Beach Girl*. This disturbing factor became so strong that he was unable to continue painting his "dream girl" until he had started *Angora Cat*, which kept coming between him and her so persistently that he had to give them both equal attention. Painting them thenceforth intermittently, he completed them together.

In the picture the cat is stretching herself comfortably and dominating the love-seat, a piece of furniture such as never existed in this world. It levitates like a magic carpet, tipping unsteadily. One leg is already in view, and it would not be surprising if it gradually arose and moved out of the picture altogether. But through all of this, the cat's composure is unruffled. The absence of any floorline increases the illusion of levitation. The humor and mystery of the picture owe much to this remarkable couch.

The position of the cat in relation to the couch is the same as the picture-frame in relation to the couch. The cat and the frame maintain an even keel, regardless of whatever position the couch may take. This incredible love-seat is upholstered in blue green phosphorescence and is framed with a sulphurous yellow, diffused neon-like light which bends around the animal.

The lines of the couch enclose the cat, and the upholstery is compositionally divided into segments of interesting shapes which lock the animal in place. By pictorial means the stability of the cat is established, an equilibrium which cannot be disturbed.

Like a luminous dial on a clock in the night, the plant emerges from out of the shadow of the background. Obligingly it withdraws its foliage to make room for the extending arm of the couch.

The upper rim of the seat in turn caresses the cat, and as an added gesture of consideration, a small flap, the elbow-rest, drops over the chair for her head to rest against.

Dynamics in the picture are centered around a series of circular movements expanding in size like those in still water after a pebble is dropped. The gleaming orbs of the cat start the cycle. These are heavily encircled in black. Next is the shadow around the face of the cat. From here on the rings of enlarging movements are modified by variations in shape. The movement spreads to the corona of darkness surrounding the body, and here begins a series of vibrations of lights and darks varying in intensity, expanding across the couch-frame, finally merging with the sea-green background.

The cat is a symbol of femininity and above it on a small wall bracket is a lion, a masculine symbol. This lion, like the face of the *Beach Girl*, was on an old canvas before Hirshfield painted over it, but while the girl's face became the focal point of the picture, the lion is relegated to the background, only to emerge as a personally conceived image in the painting *Lion*.

Lion

IN A land that seems endless, stands the lion of Judah surrounded by strange desert plants. A shimmering nile green sky falls diagonally toward the lion and merges with the landscape.

The lion's gentle and quizzical countenance, his humanized features, as well as the ashen and reddish blonde coloring in the area of the face, suggest that this is perhaps an unconscious self-portrait.

The custom-tailored mane of the lion is a snug-fitting furpiece. It frames

26

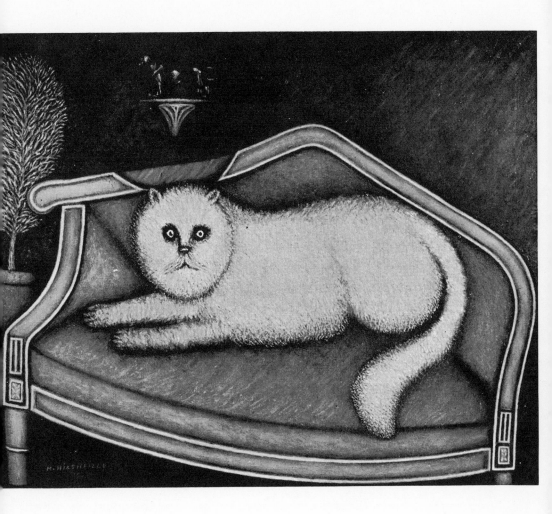

HIRSHFIELD *Angora Cat.* 1937

his face in the shape of a heart. Hirshfield's occupational background in the cloak and suit industry plays its part in the fashioning of this neckpiece. Especially does habit enter into the way the neckpiece is overlapped. This follows the feminine fashion of closing from right to left on the wearer; as a result our lion wears his furpiece contrary to the dictates of mannish attire, which decree that the overlap shall be from left to right.

Religious memories also come through. The color, and moreover the texture of the mane, resemble the gilt embroideries on Torah velvets.*

The gentleness of the man himself shows in his considerate handling of details. Each shrub is given its place under the sun and is secure. Unwilling to disturb a single green, Hirshfield curves the tail of the lion around the bush. One feels that just as the lion has avoided stepping on the bush that stands between his feet, neither will he ever trample upon any of the other bushes. For his feet are so small that should he move he could set them down between the bushes without fear of harming them.

It is precisely to give the feeling of gentleness that Hirshfield has scaled down the proportions of the legs and paws, and the effect achieved is consistent with this prominent aspect of the picture. In all of his paintings he reduces the scale of hands and feet, and in each instance, as in this, the psychological effect complements a major pictorial idea.

A striking quality in the work of Hirshfield is his use of curvilinear form. In the lion, the sweeping curves converge toward or radiate from the general area where the tail joins the body. A balance in visual and emotional interest is struck between the active linear rhythms here and the quiet ones which shape the heart of the face and the contour of the mane.

The herringbone pattern, again a vocational reminiscence, has been used throughout the painting. The oblique stripes in the sky and those on the lion's back come together to make one set; others are those in the lion's body and hind leg; the folds of the mane; and the bushes as a whole consist of countless minor variations on this herringbone theme. Projected in several directions, these converging rhythms create an undercurrent of dynamics in the predominantly passive scene.

* The Torah or Old Testament occupies a singularly hallowed place in Hebrew ritual. It is a large hand-lettered scroll with its own floridly embossed velvet sheath.

SHFIELD *Lion.* 1939

"MODEL" for *Lion*, reproduced above.

Tiger

WHEN HIRSHFIELD set out to paint his *Lion*, he used as a model the illustration of a ferocious animal titled King of Beasts, referred to previously. The picture when finished turned out, as we have seen, to be one showing the lion as a mild and gentle creature. On the way it had become a portrayal of himself and the desire to paint a ferocious animal had been submerged. But not for long, for no sooner was *Lion* completed than Hirshfield began to paint another animal picture, this time, *Tiger*.

Upon first seeing the picture, one is struck by the fact that it is a repetition of the *Lion* composition, an animal facing left in a landscape underneath a wide expanse of sky. But when comparing it with *Lion*, and now being aware of the circumstances under which both were created, it seems an inevitable consequence of frustration. For as Hirshfield would explain it, the tiger is after all actually taking the place of the lion.

And so we have *Tiger*, which Hirshfield has endowed with all the brute power he was unable to give to *Lion*. A snarling aroused beast replaces the benign lion, and the very environment reacts to his aggressive force.

The tiger's sharp pointed features, bared fangs, hypnotic eyes, heavy facial markings are in direct opposition to the countenance of the lion. The pointed ears which stand away from his head are on the alert, while the lion's ears are nestled in his mane. Our lion steps cautiously about the dense shrubbery, but the tiger, whose paws are twice the size and are equipped with large claws, has no obstacles of this nature under his feet to beset his path. Ironically enough, the lion is free to move about in his landscape but has not the will to do so, whereas the tiger, bristling with energy, is caged in by the hills on either side and by the floral barrier in the foreground. Hirshfield's zoo precludes the use of steel bars.

The mellow colors in *Lion* are changed here to stinging tones of acid quality. The clouds no longer descend like a gentle mist, but radiate in extreme agitation from behind the tiger's head. The flamelike stripings on the animal heighten the feeling of excitement, and a tortuous note is added by the hills

HARSHFIELD *Tiger*. 1940   Collection The Museum of Modern Art.

that frame the animal on either side, for these hills, lined with red veinlike markings, convolute like viscera.

Finally, as a telling stroke, Hirshfield has created scale by juxtaposing three tiny birds in a tree to the tiger, and in this way intensifies the stature and vitality of the beast.

Since *Lion* is in the image of the artist as we know him, one wonders if *Tiger* is not perhaps a symbolic "Portrait of the Artist as a Young Man."

Girl in the Mirror

LE REVE by Rousseau had been bothering Hirshfield. He had no consciousness of the relation between his own creative activity and that of Rousseau. He had no knowledge of the Douanier's place in the world of art; the poetry of Rousseau had not reached him. Here was a painting, and this was his direct reaction to it.

He felt it was not bad, not bad at all, but the "swollen" contours of the nude who dreamed she had been transported to the jungle on a red sofa, disturbed him. He said so on several occasions, and finally volunteered to change these contours. The spirit in which he did this brought to mind the

32

story of Rousseau's reaction upon seeing his first Cezanne. If Cezanne would only let him finish it!

Hirshfield mentioned that he was in search of subject matter for his next picture. Without realizing it he wanted to paint a nude; but the entire nature of the situation indicated this was one time when the artist needed the suggestion to come from without. Sensing this, my wife casually suggested that he paint a nude, and his response was quick and warm. He was immediately diverted from his desire to alter the Rousseau. When asked if he would paint from a model, he replied, naturally, no, it wouldn't be proper at his age, 69, but he had a good idea of what he wanted to do.

Three months later, Hirshfield's *Girl in the Mirror* was completed.

In showing the canvas to me for the first time, he emphasized that while artists generally painted the front view of nudes, he considered the back view even more beautiful. With pride he called attention to the anatomical details, especially in the legs and feet, which he felt were "better than a camera could do." He also took pleasure in the way he had done the decorations on the mirror and small table, which "look just like mother-of-pearl inlay."

I suddenly noticed that Mrs. Hirshfield had quietly retired from the room. While admiring the textures, I had run my fingers over the built-up pigments which were modeled on the buttocks of the nude, little suspecting that it would disturb anyone.

This kind of modesty, an aspect of Hirshfield's social environment to which he still conformed, had been at play from the very beginning. It accounted for his original difficulty in choosing subject matter for this painting, and his decision to do a nude only after approval from others. It was responsible, regardless of the economic factor, for his attitude in avoiding the use of a model, and finally it was at the basis of the painting's entire concept.

Upon looking at the picture we find it does violence to the laws of optics. Turned from the observer, the girl is facing the mirror but her reflection does not return as a front view. The full sweep of the girl's hair repeats in the mirror and the right arm caressing it swings surprisingly to the extreme left. Hirshfield has ingeniously opened the reflection like a door away from her.

This unorthodox way of making a reflection would appear to be subconsciously prompted by the desire to avoid any presentation of the front view of the nude. The technique for accomplishing this comes from habits formed in Hirshfield's former craft, for the nude and the mirror image open up exactly as doubled-over cloth does when cut for the back of a garment, for instance.

The vase on the tabouret, pale blue and emerging phantom-like out of the dark, paraphrases the contours of the nude. A tiara of greens and flowers sprays from the vase and reaches over the frame of the mirror to act as a shield. By the significant placing of this lacy fern, an intuitive allusion to a front view is made. The use of this poetic symbol is as close as Hirshfield could come at this time to readjustment of his sense of modesty from a lay environment to that of the artist.

In painting this still-life, it apparently seemed impossible to Hirshfield that a round vase could stand on a round table in a picture, and we know they are round for the ovals of both vase-top and table-top are shown. The bottom of the vase is presented, then, not by a curved base, but by straight lines. With this firm foundation for the vase, we are thus assured it will not rock and consequently the extensive spray of foliage and flowers will not move from its appointed place. In doing this, Hirshfield has employed, though quite unawarely, two viewpoints, one focused on the base of the vase at eye level, and the other on the vase-top and table-top below eye level. In Cubism this is referred to as circulating viewpoint.

The mother-of-pearl inlay which Hirshfield loved is the motif for the pearly flesh tones of the nude. Against the pearly tints are contrasted gunmetal greys and blacks. These contrasts form the basis for the color orchestration, while the higher color notes of the moonstone blue vase and green sprays play a countermelody to the larger tonal values.

Curvilinear rhythms ply in and out of the mirror, and together with the rhythms made by the gestures of the arms, are paced to occur at intervals which most effectively aid the composition. The right arm takes its position to the extreme left in the mirror, but the hand with the powderpuff is not reflected at all. We have but to consider the confusion a fourth arm would cause to realize how wise was its omission.

34

HIRSHFIELD *Girl in the Mirror.* 1940 Collection The Museum of Modern Art.

Through the necessity of presenting the reflection as he did, Hirshfield has found his own way to create space. Unbroken by a floor line, the mottled floor and wall are one. A deep rich grey continues uninterrupted from the floor, up around the mirror, to the top of the painting. The graining which patterns this floor also continues up the wall. The directional movement caused by the pattern creates a receding space, a curved plane like the inside of a sphere. The table and the nude which stand on the floor and the frame which hangs on the wall, are all on this same curved plane.

An illusion of deep space is created against this plane by the mirror itself, for the artist has cut it out like a window in his wall, and it is in this opening that the reflection swings away. He conceives of the reflection in the mirror as actually being deeper in space than anything in the room.

In this unique concept, the demarcation between the curved plane as foreground and the space in the mirror as background, is suggested by the horizontal line at the bottom of the mirror.

As shown throughout this analysis, though the reflection may be illogical optically, it functions logically from the pictorial standpoint and it solves the psychological problem which the artist faced in painting a nude.

Necessarily linked to the pictorial treatment of the reflection is Hirshfield's answer to the question of balance. The picture is based on simple bi-symmetry, but one side, instead of being a repetition of the other, is a compensation for it, and herein the creativeness of the artist plays its role. The reflection is placed slightly higher than the nude; the graining of the hair in both figures runs in the same direction although the profiles are opposite each other; the curves on the form in the mirror are a variation of those on the girl in front of it. To compensate for cutting off the reflection at the mirror base, the striking still-life is introduced below. Not only is the vase which appears in this still-life an ageless symbol for the body of a woman, but the emotional significance of this unit counterbalances that of the nude.

Although the reduced scale of the arms and hands, and especially the streamlined version of the reflection in the mirror, make her seem a creature of the Cenozoic age, she is more than likely a lorelei out of Hirshfield's dream mythology.

36

Nude at the Window

NUDE AT THE WINDOW* was painted directly after Hirshfield had completed *Girl in the Mirror*, and it is an interesting commentary on the evolution of his own attitudes that he was now able to give a forthright portrayal of a nude. Intuitively, he has come to understand that the nature of the subject matter itself is subordinate to the higher morality of the creation of a work of art, and this undoubtedly enabled him to overcome his former reticence.

Like a dazzling apparition, this ivory pink creature with yellow blonde hair emerges from the mysterious black depths which we know are no more than

* The artist's full title is *Nude at the Window: Hot Night in July*.

37

the interior of a darkened room. The brilliant red drapes striped with black and yellow are gently held aside by one hand, and the other drape responds before it is touched as if she controlled it magically.

Around her, the darkened room which is her background takes on the contour of a huge black vase, and at the top of the vase a valance with two pendants appears. The figure within levitates above exquisitely designed slippers which are themselves suspended. The whole is like a reincarnation in a funerary urn.

The vase, as in *Girl in the Mirror*, may be considered a significant, subconsciously achieved form. In each, it paraphrases the human form, but here it is no longer separated from the nude figure. Merged into a single image, it confirms the homogeneous character of the painter's present attitude.

The outline contours of the nude are conceived as a set of two continuous curving lines, and these play an important role in the picture. One begins under the arm, follows down around the torso and legs, taking in the sweep of the abdomen in an oyster-shaped arc on the way, and ends under the other arm.

An interesting anatomical variation is the rendering of one thigh in profile, the other in front view.

The other continuous line, starting and ending at the chest, encompasses the breasts, arms and head. Divided into two sections, then, the nude consists of two forms delineated by flowing lines and set upon each other; and the forms are tacked in place at the breasts. Scallops bordering the drapes compulsively repeat this latter motif, interrupted but briefly by the introduction of the hand and momentarily displaced to make room for the foot. The repeating lines of the drapes which surround the nude, complement its curvilinear rhythms and are like magnetic currents emanating from the figure.

HIRSHFIELD *Nude at the Window.* 1941

WILLIAM DORIANI with *Lincoln and Roosevel*

CHAPTER THREE

WILLIAM DORIANI

At the height of a successful operatic career, the tenor Doriani felt a strong urge to paint. Abashed by such an idea, he was unable to bring himself to a point where he could begin. He was even unable to face the paint-store man, and invented a nephew for whom he was buying supplies. In this way he succeeded in obtaining the necessary equipment without involving himself in any way.

But the bare canvas was too forbidding. He was unable to place a stroke upon it. This state of affairs continued until one night he had a dream, in the midst of which a group of ancient men, in robes befitting great scholars, appeared before him "like a revelation." The foremost of the group implanted in the hand of Doriani a brush and palette.

Awakening—it was in the small hours of the night—he grasped his brushes and colors and set upon the task of making his first picture. No longer afraid, he painted with perfect confidence and freedom. By daybreak he had finished. It was a small canvas on which a toe dancer was poised before a fascinated audience. He signed it "W. Doriani, 27, 1, 1931, #1."*

Exhausted by his efforts, he retired and slept, undisturbed by the cries of his family, who were startled that morning to find a freshly painted picture before them.

Doriani continued to paint, numbering each picture alongside his signature, as it was completed. This was in Europe during the early '30's. He was unable to show his work publicly, although several friends encouraged him to continue to paint. At one time, he approached a well-known painter with the thought of receiving art instruction. The painter, upon examining Doriani's work, exclaimed admiringly, "You have something I could never give you." Doriani was fortunate in having approached a man who understood that it was important not to tamper with the mechanism by which this self-taught artist worked. Formal art instruction might have increased his skill, but it would no doubt have blunted the edge of his spontaneity with the result that his work might have become self-conscious and dull.

Not until several years later and after he had returned to America, did he show his works publicly. The occasion was the Washington Square Outdoor Art Mart, which is held twice yearly in Greenwich Village, and it was here that I first saw them. There were a score strung along a cellar

* Doriani's birthday is January 27.

guard-rail on MacDougal Street, blowing in the wind, ragged-edged and unframed, but indomitably gay and sparkling. To be confronted suddenly by so vital a painting expression was as thrilling as it was unexpected, each picture speaking in its own way, one intimately, one with gaiety, another in frolicsome good humor. But I could not risk facing the artist who I felt was close at hand. He might dispel the illusion or temper the warmth of my intimacy with the pictures. I walked away to return again and again. And finally I turned and spoke to him. He was just like his pictures.

Several months later, a one-man show was arranged for Doriani with the Marie Harriman Gallery, and it opened there on March 13th, 1939. At this time the critics lauded his work; Henry McBride of *The Sun* found that "Mr. Doriani has a natural instinct for picture-making. He is perfectly fearless in his use of color and seldom makes mistakes. He is equally unabashed in his use of composition. . . . On opening day, it was not surprising to see the visitors beaming with friendliness at the naive but thoroughly entertaining pictures of the newcomer."

The following quotations are from the author's foreword to the exhibition:

William Doriani, born in the Ukraine 49 years ago, came to America when a boy, remaining until after he had become a naturalized citizen. He then returned to the Continent to study music in Italy and Russia. After a successful operatic career in Europe as a tenor, he began to paint, creating his first picture on his 40th birthday.

His musical talent had been cultivated by intensive study, but his painting talent remains self-taught. Whereas the world of music had long been his milieu, he had never visited a museum or an art exhibition. This preserved for him intact the particular kind of intuitive seeing requisite to his manner of expression, for he is in the tradition of those painters who find their solution independent of historical knowledge of art or experience with the painting of others.

The use of unorthodox plastic devices and the ingenuousness of the drawing may lead the observer to compare Doriani's expression with the creative work of children. But juxtaposed to child-painting, his work may readily be seen to be on the complex adult level of mental, emotional, and physical coordination. Rather does he use these as qualities common to folk-art, together with the ingratiating awkwardness of his humor, the density of his colors, the employing of tactile qualities of homely objects. Even the squat figures have the look, essentially through the scale on which they are drawn, of characters out of folklore.

The paintings of Doriani are transmutations of his love for the theatre, nature, the U.S.A., and his relish for the gamut of human types and temperaments, which he portrays with an irrepressible and infectious gaiety of spirit.

42

By this time fifteen of his paintings had found their way into collections, and reproductions of his work began to appear in newspapers and magazines. Doriani was pleased and painted several interesting large oils.

But a series of unhappy circumstances made it impossible for him to continue for long. His son lost his job and the proceeds of Doriani's new-found recognition went to provide food and shelter. Unable to get an audience for his singing talent, and having no extra money to spend for materials, he stopped painting. He has repeatedly said that not to paint is to suffer, but he had to suffer. Friends came to his aid by buying what pictures they could, but he was unable in this way to support his family and resume painting.

However, after many months away from his easel, Doriani has now been assigned to the WPA Art Project, where he is busily engaged in painting again.

Today in the tenth year of his painting career, he has completed 80 canvases, and a group of black and white drawings which are as rich and varied in their color tonalities as are his oils.

In view of his career, it is not surprising that Doriani should have painted many oils revealing interesting aspects of the stage. He loves to tell of one of his first experiences with "picture-making," something that happened in the theatre. It proved to be one of those tentative efforts by which a latent talent rises to the surface. He was on tour, and arriving at his destination, proceeded to the concert hall. His sense of fun prompted him to try to get in without his credentials. The stage-door keeper would not let him pass. Doriani took a pad and pencil from his pocket, and engaging in a running conversation, began to sketch, never taking his eyes off his subject, never glancing at the paper. As he continued to sketch in this way, he struck a deal with the guard: "I'm sketching you and if it looks like you, you can have it. In exchange, will you let me in?" The guard agreed, and finally when Doriani felt he had finished, he looked at his sketch and to his amazement found what seemed to be a striking resemblance. Naturally he could not get himself to surrender it, and so it is unknown to this day whether or not he talked his way in to sing that night.

In the paintings that follow, it will be seen that this playful humor makes itself felt at every turn.

43

Toe Dancer

THIS IS Doriani's first painting, and appropriately enough, it is of the stage. *Toe Dancer* depicts the danseuse *sur-les-points*, calmly poised and facing an enthralled audience.

By surprisingly simple handling, Doriani has managed subtly to guide the eye of the observer. This eye path is often achieved by artists through various painting devices. In *Toe Dancer*, it is done by psychological emphasis. While there are more than a score of figures in the picture, all feet have been omitted with the exception of a single pair, those of the dancer, which are covered by vermilion slippers, the brightest color spots in the canvas. Neither are there hands visible, to interrupt the concentration upon the dancer's toes, and the eye is firmly focused at this point.

A rapport between the dancer and her audience is established plastically in the picture. The diagonal line caused by the heads of the audience is carried out of the picture by the slant of the stage. Oblique lines in the opposite direction recur in the torsos of the audience, making an excellent foil for the main vertical, the dancer.

The picture has the textures of old parchment and leather, especially in the deep ivory-colored background, which has the character of Novgorod icons. Against the ivory background, Doriani has kept the color key of the audience essentially within a range of light and dark tans, browns and blacks, but on the stage there is a color pick-up which acts as lighting. The gay green of the dancer's costume, together with this surrounding lighted area, are so concentrated as to elevate the stage beyond the pale of the audience.

Doriani's kindly attitude toward life imparts to all of his figures a gentle humanity. The awkwardness of his drawing endows his figures with a folk quality, and the Giottoesque huddling gives them intimacy.

Because they create an expressiveness that is direct, fresh and humorous. his limitations in technique no longer remain handicaps.

RIANI *Toe Dancer.* 1931

DORIANI *Flag Day.* 1935

Flag Day

AFTER SPENDING thirteen years in Europe, Doriani returned to his beloved America. He arrived on Flag Day. The impact of the occasion was so great that he had to commemorate it in paint. The long line of the parade undoubtedly influenced his choice of a canvas—his painting is three times as wide as it is high. This horizontal canvas reciprocates by enhancing the general movement of the march in his picture.

The painting is divided into three horizontal bands which extend across the canvas. In the lower one are the marching feet. The middle band is made up of the heads and flags, and in the topmost row are the blooms.

Each boy in the foreground seems possessed of many legs, upon one of which he stands, the rest being in progressively rising positions. The legs move, yet the boys remain before us, as though they were in continuous motion upon a treadmill.

But if the boys remain, still the movement of the parade is taken up by the eye as it travels forward along the stripes of each flag, rests for an instant, and leaps to the next, until it passes along the entire width of the canvas. The flowers, in double file, keep pace with the procession of flags.

Where Doriani may have consciously hoped to attain forward movement in painting the marching feet, he succeeded only in creating a treadmill, but in the two upper horizontal bands, the flags and the blooms, where movement was not his intention, he succeeded in producing a forward motion.

Colors are juicy and resonant, and are applied in heavy pigment. They shine forth with great vigor and intensity. In the procession of color that passes before the eyes, the red, white and blue of the flags are first to be seen. The repetition of black caps and black uniforms of the boys is uninterrupted except for the deep royal blue stockings. All of this moves in front of an olive green background, into which the large deep orange yellow blossoms are introduced. These last are borderline color notes rescued and kept in line by the accompanying greens of the shrubs upon which they grow.

Doriani's respect for the flag is evidenced in the careful way he has given it exact detail. Although there are many more than a score of flags, the thirteen stripes of each are visible, and the forty-eight stars clearly indicated. The hat of each boy covers some part of the blue field, yet in no flag does it do so sufficiently to hide the horizontal row of eight stars or the vertical row of six, which visually suggest the total number of stars.

If the marchers resemble French school boys doing the German goose-step, it is immaterial, for the flags they carry are unmistakable.

Rehearsal

WHAT IS it in the work of Doriani that brings a smile to the lips of the observer? The rehearsal is undoubtedly serious business, yet Doriani has given to all of his characters his own humorous appraisal of their doings.

The man holding the score of the opera is Doriani. Planted squarely as a focus for all activity, he is surrounded by animated and slightly unsteady personages.

The informality of a rehearsal is the keynote of the painting, and everyone is engaged in the business of polishing up his own part. Assisted by his wife, Doriani is reading a score carefully marked "Rigoletto—G. Verdi." The big burly impresario who stands in the foreground like a traffic cop, shows his dictatorial hand. The dancer, spinning like a top, goes through her routine. Literally at her elbow are comb, powderpuff, mirror, rouge.

On the other side, the clown, sitting on his hands, also has his make-up kit, mirror and puff, and the violinist his violin case. These objects rise obliquely into the picture and direct the eye to the upward movement of the N composition which the figures make. The manner in which they steer the eye into the composition brings to mind a Degas rehearsal painting in which he used string instruments for the same purpose. Pre-candid-camera Degas got the idea for these remarkable effects from photographs that were generally regarded as compositional mistakes made by the primitives in photography. It is noteworthy that Doriani, knowing nothing of Degas and less about photography, composed these objects instinctively.

All of the figures are dark accents placed against flat background areas of luggage tan and fuchsia, grey and mahogany. Two vivid color notes in the figures are opposed to each other, the dress of the dancer in which hues blend from orange to rose, and the bright green trousers of the clown. This green on one side and the orange rose on the other form the base points of the letter N made by the figures in the composition.

Paralleling the bended line of the bow, the violin extends along the steam pipe, and the radiator attaches itself to it, as if it were a fantastic musical instrument. One may sense that when the violinist plays, the notes will be

ANI *Rehearsal.* 1931

amplified through the vertical pipes of the radiator, and aural effects combining the bow on the strings and radiator percussion will produce the bizarre music of a new instrument, the violin-calliope.

Theatre

THEATRE is one of Doriani's most daring and unorthodox canvases. The unusual and arresting execution is a very reasonable and delightful solution in keeping with the artist's basic idea, which is to show a comedian on the stage and the hilarious response of the audience to his antics.

By a simple piece of "business" quite like that of an actor who steps out of character and back into it again, Doriani has given his experience with the theatre. He presents it from three viewpoints, backstage, upon the stage, and from the audience. First he paints the actor, curtains and upper boxes as seen from the wings. Still in character, he now "goes on" to paint the audience from the stage. Then, stepping out of character and into the audience, he gives through a series of contrasting stripes, the view of the platform elevation of the stage from there.

It is a gala occasion. The boxes, ornamented with gilt floral motifs, are garlands strung along the theatre, from which smiling faces pop up as fresh as daisies out of window boxes.

In the orchestra, the rug is patterned with confetti-like sprinklings of color. Against this background is the main body of the audience. It is a commentary on the ability of the comedian that he has "laid them out flat" with laughter. The prone position of his audience is accentuated as Doriani carefully shows the entire figure of each spectator, dovetailing them to fit. For example, the feet of the man in the center row, aisle seat, are placed so as not to disturb the people in front of him. The green-striped stage curtain falls in huge folds, barely touches the actor's head and rests there like a grossly exaggerated and clownish turban or fez.

The practise of isolating objects so that they remain free of each other, or of allowing them barely to touch but not overlap, is one very frequently used

50

ANI *Theatre.* 1934 Collection Georges Keller.

by self-taught artists. In *Theatre*, Doriani does this always in a humorous vein, basically because of his own spirit of fun. Hirshfield, whom we have seen to paint this way very deliberately, achieves psychological effects thereby. In *Tiger*, the tree retreats or shrinks from the menacing claw, emphasizing the ferocity of the beast. In *Lion*, paws and bushes are again used, this time to obtain the opposite effect, that of gentleness. Here the paws are reduced so as not to trample (or overlap) the bushes.

In *Theatre*, the figures in the audience form a flat rectangular area of lights and darks and they are arranged to suggest a multicolored checkerboard in which each square is given its special color and function. Despite the surprising conception, they face in the normal way, at right angles to the stage. The actor on the stage manipulates the game; by virtue of knowing his audience, he is able to control their reactions. It is true they respond to him heartily, yet they are not looking at him but at the artist who is painting the picture. Doriani, as painter, is still the actor holding his audience.

"Laying out" the audience is an unconscious achievement, as much a part of the plastic means as it is of the underlying humor. For this same two-dimensional quality exists in all of Doriani's works. To comply with it, the side of the stage, as we have already seen, is also flattened.

It is interesting to note the difference in the way he has created a rapport between performer and audience in *Theatre* and in *Toe Dancer*. The oblique composition of *Toe Dancer* creates tension and hushed abeyance, while the horizontals in *Theatre* make for ease and free abandon.

The theatre is customarily one of the mainstays of urban life, but Doriani has filled it with folk-like figures, and the colors, orange, brilliant greens, tan yellow, light blue and pinks, remind one of the gaiety of coloring in peasant costumes worn on festive occasions.

The actor and the curtain are perhaps the clearest painting passages in the composition. This is probably a reflection of Doriani's love for the stage and his attitude toward those who tread upon it.

52

CHAPTER FOUR

PATRICK J. SULLIVAN

THE IDEA behind the Society of Independent Artists is a vital one. This group always has the welcome sign in full view and artists from all over the country and from other parts of the world as well avail themselves of the opportunity to show their work. There is no jury to cull the "good" from the

53

"bad" and leave only safe mediocrity. The public may make its own selection and decide for itself what is good or bad. This has always been stimulating to me and I never miss an Independent show. One could wish for better lighting and less crowding of pictures, but if this makes for some hardship, it is still worth it.

In the Spring of 1937, in a particularly dim corner of the section which housed the letter S, I found a frameless canvas, so forceful and so striking that I had great difficulty containing myself. My wife and brother were with me at the time, and so provocative was the picture that I began talking very rapidly about it. It proved to be like an interminable ball of wool—having begun to pull the yarn, I was unable to find an end to it.

The picture, medium sized, was a densely wooded scene with trees whose foliage was like broccoli. Ashen lights played upon it. Figures engaged in symbolic activities occupied the foreground, and through the trunks of the trees, as if passing through the mazes of the mind, one could see the light of day off in the distance. Dramatic and intense, the painting revealed a profoundly mature pictorial means. It was intriguingly titled *Man's Procrastinating Pastime* and was signed P. J. Sullivan. The secretary said his address was Wheeling, W. Va.

I wrote Sullivan and learned from him that this was his first painting, and after an exchange of correspondence I purchased it. The picture grew stronger as I lived with it. Still I was unable to uncover all of the hidden symbolism, and one day Sullivan called me to account for not having inquired as to the theme, which he would send to me if I was interested. Naturally I was.

Sullivan conceives of the themes of his paintings as an extension of the paintings themselves. Graphically written, they are an enrichment of the esthetic experience. In the discussions that follow the "theme" of each painting is quoted in full.

Similarly his letters constitute an invaluable source of information, for they reveal his character and integrity, his ideas and ideals. They are in themselves a vivid human document, and it is only through insufficient space that mere excerpts will be published here.

54

HISTORY: P. J. SULLIVAN

Born in Braddock, Pa., March 17, 1894. (It is obvious why my first or christian name is Patrick). My father Redmond Sullivan, my mother Mary (nee) Downing, both Irish. My father was born in Ireland and my mother in England. My maternal grandfather was an architect. My father a farmer and later in this country a steel worker.

My father died when I was two years old leaving five children. There were twelve altogether myself the youngest. When father died, my mother was very ill necessitating a long stay in a Pittsburgh hospital and being without funds, mother, before going to the hospital placed me in an orphan home where I remained until the age of fifteen. In the orphan home I worked in the printing shop. This work first gave me the idea of dabbling in painting, but I never gave much time to it other than sketching what everyone thought meaningless stuff.

Upon leaving the orphans home at fifteen, I went to McKeesport, Pa., secured a job in the sheet-iron mill there and mother and I set up housekeeping. After a year and a half at McKeesport, I and mother (or should I say mother and I, I arrived first) came to Wheeling, W. Va. I worked here a short while in the mills and later secured a position as an assistant playground manager of the Wheeling playgrounds. It was on the playgrounds that I first started to paint (that is house painting). This enlivened my interest in fine art again. I'd paint pictures on heavy paper, cardboard, old window blinds or what have you. Some I'd destroy later and some were lost, strayed or stolen.

In 1916 I enlisted in the Army. Served a few months on the Mexican border. After the U. S. got into the big squabble, I was made a Cadre (instructor) officer and did much in the way of organizing the new army. I also was a top sergeant in the regular army. I had charge (under other officers, of course) of the Bush-Terminal Docks at South Brooklyn during the closing month of the war. We handled the shipping of troops and supplies.

I was discharged March 1919. Came back to Wheeling, worked another year at the playgrounds, left that job and secured a job with the American Railway Express Co. Met my wife there, she worked in the office. I married in March 1920 and took up the house-painting trade in earnest. Worked my apprenticeship under a Frenchman by the name of James De-Shon.

To digress a moment—I once copied Hoffman "Christ at Twelve" in the temple. This painting of Hoffman I always considered effeminate. Anyhow I copied it on a common tea towel with left-overs from house jobs. In my copy I made the nose longer (more like a Hebraic nose) I made the shoulders more rugged looking and I put just a tinge of the "Adam's apple" in the neck. In short I made a good-looking masculine Christ-child. (I certainly do not like an effeminate-looking Christ.)

During the depression I had much time to paint and that's how I spent my spare time. Believe it or not, *Man's Procrastinating Pastime* is my first all original canvass.

A few months ago I worked on the Ethiopian affair that is prior to the start of that war. After I was getting along with the picture, I got work and couldn't work at it much and the war was shortly over and I became enraged and ripped the canvass to pieces. In that picture I had a large Ethiopian in a fighting attitude with an out-moded rifle. On the other end of the canvass a modern fighting Roman and behind him, tanks, air-

55

planes and other modern war equipment. In the clouds over the Roman soldier I showed a vision of Caeser and over the Ethiopian in the clouds a vision of Solomon. I was going to title the picture: "Will the spirit of Solomon or Caeser prevail."

I never run out of ideas to paint. I don't care for some, or should I say, most of the so-called modern art.

It's all rather crude, I think, that is from a technical point of view. If one must paint pictures I say paint them so that they can be viewed from any angle or distance and look clean and plain. That's what I call art. The old masters painted that way.

I buried a boy. I have two daughters one 14 the other 12. The youngest likes art and I think she will take it up.

I never took an art lesson in my life. I just like to paint and from now on I shall paint things that come to mind—powerful stuff that will make people think—that's my goal.

P. S. I might add that my maternal grandmother was a cousin of John Redmond (now deceased) leader of Irish Parliament and leader of the famous Princess Pat's regiment. He also was the father of the Home Rule Bill for Ireland. This grandmother of mine was a Redmond of Wexford Ireland.

As Sullivan points out in his "history," he turned during the enforced leisure of the depression, from house-painting to picture-painting. Because his methodical technique was slow and deliberate, he sometimes required a year to complete a picture.

His first opportunity to show publicly came in 1938 when the Museum of Modern Art included all three pictures he had made up to then in their showing of *Masters of Popular Painting*. At that time, the effect that exhibiting would have upon this artist filled me with concern. Deciding that it would not affect him adversely, I wrote in the catalogue to the exhibition:

By the time the third painting arrived it was quite evident that the particular primitive quality which distinguished this artist's work was deeply embedded in his personality, and that, similarly, when the time came, the wide step from the shelter of carefully considered individual encouragement to a position before public appraisal would be made without disturbance to his untouched spirit.

And this is essentially my attitude toward this question in relation to all of the painters in the book.

Sullivan brought his wife to New York to see the exhibition, and when Mrs. Sullivan, who is very sympathetic and understanding about his painting efforts, saw her husband's work on display, she wept. Later she admitted that seeing his paintings for the first time "beautifully framed and hanging in a museum" was too much joy for her. Never having seen one of his pic-

56

tures framed, she said, "The frames sort of accentuate the canvases or sort of magnify them."

They brought to the exhibition a World War "buddy" who was a lieutenant on the New York police force. This officer seemed duly impressed with his old friend's work, but tired rather quickly. When Sullivan called this to his attention, he confessed this was the "first art gallery" he had ever been in. While in New York, they visited the Statue of Liberty, Grant's Tomb, Radio City; they rode on the top of a bus, sat in the Mayor's chair at City Hall, and had their first swim in the ocean.

After Sullivan returned home, he often referred to his visit to the museum show. Some of his reactions to the other painters, which were interspersed throughout his letters, follow:

John Kane was surely great for detail.

Hicks' "The Peaceable Kingdom" is the only one among all that contains symbolism to a small degree.

I like Rousseau's work very much. He certainly was realistic in its truest sense. He surely felt his work. It shows it. I imagine he liked his jungle canvases better than all the others.

Peyronnet was a careful painter. His work in lithography was probably responsible for the clear-cut work he turned out.

Bombois' looks very much like school work. That is, it smacks of training. Some of the figures look sort of stilted. He gets good perspective.

And of newspaper criticism he wrote:

Proof that they don't grasp my work is shown in the article in which he stated "The weird strange imaginative qualities of Pippin and Sullivan make a distinct impression." This writer doesn't go into the work at all. I think he really doesn't understand it thematically or otherwise. But perhaps he'll tumble later on when he really sees the work instead of just looking at it.

Upon seeing a painting by Dali for the first time:

This man is a master of the hidden theme.

In December of 1938 we visited the Sullivans, and prior to our trip, Mrs. Sullivan wrote:

You would enjoy seeing Mr. Sullivan's studio, we always kid him about. But perhaps some day he can have a room of his own to do his art work. He surely loves to paint. He puts his heart and soul in it. And myself, I suppose I get all the thrills from it.

We were naturally curious to see the "studio." It was, as she had told us, a corner of their bedroom. In the center was the large heating stove, and near it were two kitchen chairs, one serving as an easel and the other as seat for the artist. A floor lamp stood nearby and on the "easel" was the picture *Haunts in the Totalitarian Woods* which he was doing at the time. In this corner Sullivan creates his profoundly evocative pictures.

He uses five-and-ten-cent-store brushes and mixes his own colors.

I use pure colors ground in oil, triple ground. Using pure linseed oil fresh daily.

When his paintings are finished and dry, he sandpapers the built-up pigments, following the movement of the brush strokes. In this way he is able to modulate the relief-surfaces. And finally he varnishes his canvas with flat varnish, which gives it its waxen tone.

During the day we spent with them, the Sullivans took us to visit Mt. de Chantal Academy. He had house-painted every nook and cranny of the Academy, both inside and out. We met Sister Cecilia, who was in charge of the Art Department. She was very much interested in his paintings, eager to hear about art in New York City and very well informed about the School of Paris.

Over a period of years Sullivan has kept up a stream of letters. Here are a few more of his opinions:

Reason for Painting: "If my work helps others to think, I mean really think in the true sense of the word, then I am achieving my goal. To get anywhere without making people think doesn't interest me. My canvases will be along the same lines as *Man's Procrastinating Pastime,* impressive, profound, unusual. I want my canvases to be of the kind, that when viewed will hit them as it were and make them think and know life in its real rich fulness, its truths, for all is truth. You remember the old saying: 'A lie is the truth in disguise.' It is my intention to bring truth out in all its glory on my canvases.—if you will, a sort of parable in picture form."

Creative Impulse: "When I start on a picture I have already painted it in my mind, (visioned it). And I am of the opinion that an artist should paint it as he has seen it with his mind's eye.

"The idea of the painting came to me strongly and I just simply had to paint it.

"But nothing matters as long as I can just keep on painting. To me that is the main thing."

Philosophical Comments: "It seems to me sometimes as though a primitive is supposed to be an object of ridicule. I say to all those who make sport of the primitives or any other so-called 'naives' or whatever other pet names they have for them, I say this:

When you read books and listen to lectures you get the sense of others, but when you read men and think, then you get sense of your own.

"I tried to follow the advice the sweet old lady gave to her son when he was leaving for the big city to seek fame and fortune. She said 'Son, never try to be what you ain't. Just be what you are.' What difference does it make if this mother was ungrammatical? Her utterance was and is still a veritable gem of wisdom.

"The late A. Brisbane always said that his greatest editorial was in three words, Think, Think, Think. I try mightily to apply his favorite editorial to all five senses. Or as Channing Pollock said 'All values yield to concentration'.

"I think the articles on Doriani are fine. I read them with much interest. Whether it's about Doriani, Kane, Rousseau or what have you in the primitives, I always get the idea that the critics and the art public in general view a primitive as though he were a strange sort of being. I sometimes think they have in their minds that a primitive is an overgrown kid with the mentality of a kid, and again there are those who give this thought out. 'What does he know about art? He never took any lessons, never studied. I'd want some artist's work who has gone through art school and knows his stuff.' I think Doriani can teach many of the so-called artists plenty especially about color, and I sincerely hope that his efforts are rewarded in a manner commensurate with his very fine work."

The letter that follows records a tragic happening, a misunderstanding with deeply human overtones. It may serve to illustrate how museums can make a contribution by establishing a closer contact with exhibiting artists.

I played with the idea of entering a canvas in some museum or gallery for quite a long time. Whether a jury would admit my work intrigued me. Too, I've wondered would the press notice my work and would the patrons of art give it any attention—or would anybody notice it.

I had a good frame made for *First Law of Nature* and entered it. It was passed by a jury. Other than accepting the canvas for their show nothing else happened.

Though Mrs. Sullivan came with me—I attended the preview and of course the presentation of the medals alone. I borrowed fifty dollars to take us there. We made the trip by bus. A lot of my friends thought I was foolish in making the trip, but when you see the *come-on* invitation they sent me in the same cover the acceptance card came in you'll understand why I went. I figured the winners would not know until the presentation ceremonies actually opened in order to put over the element of surprise. Boy, was I all wet, *and how!* The invitation sure fooled a lot of artists who I suppose went to as much trouble as I did to go there, thinking perhaps as I did, that they would be winners.

However, I've learned, and the hard way. To borrow fifty dollars when one hasn't worked all winter—and what a tough winter—makes it harder still. But I've a good strong chin and I can take it, but I am not going to be on the receiving end all the time.

After a long tiresome sixteen hours on buses (we couldn't sleep like some do on the buses) we arrived exhausted. My attire was correct, good suit, overcoat, hat and etc., all but shoes. They looked a little shoddy. Out of our precious small roll I dropped in a shoe store and bought a pair for four dollars. I forgot to mention we arrived preview day about 1:30 P. M. After I put on the shoes we scouted around and finally engaged a room with a bath at a hotel, $3.00. We enjoyed a bath and I shaved, dressed carefully and we hunted up a nice place to dine after which I boarded a bus to the Museum alone—thinking of course, it (the preview) was just for the artists.

I arrived a little ahead of time. The head watchman let me in. He said: "You're early. No one here yet. However since you are an exhibitor (I introduced myself of course) come in and make yourself at home till the show opens."

He escorted me to a small office of his in the basement. He gave me a catalog. I knew what the score was immediately. I thumbed thru the catalog smiled and otherwise hid my feelings.

Directly other watchmen came in also a carpenter a checker and one of the lesser officials in formal "bib and tucker." I don't remember his name. I talked with the carpenter and a watchman. The watchmen work in the museum when there are no shows on, some as janitors, varnishers, and etc. The following is what the watchman told me:

"You know, Sullivan, when your canvas arrived, we talked about it very much. We wondered how you got the embossed effect, especially in your Adam and Eve. We (he used the pronoun) decided that there was only one way you could do it and that was to sort of mould it some way and press it on the canvas."

I have quoted this watchman verbatim. How crude, dumb and insulting. His attitude was sly with the air of one who knew all about art. He didn't ask how I accomplished the work in relief, but doped it out, as it were, to his entire satisfaction. I restrained myself and told him quietly that his knowledge of such things was nil to say the least. I informed him in plain English that to do work in relief required an absolute knowledge of paints, how to mix, when and how to apply. I told him that it would be utterly impossible to mould lead and oil to press on canvas. I suggested X-ray or other lights on the canvas to prove the utter nonsense of his (or their) ideas.

While we were talking another watchman came in. I asked him if the show had started. "Yes," he said, "just started."

There was quite a crowd mostly women in the inevitable southern belle costumes. No one paid any attention to me I didn't meet the director or anybody connected with the official family. I was like a lost sheep. There were two Negroes attending the show and I talked with them awhile. Presently the presentation was on. The Governor wasn't there nor the Mayor as was advertised. After that, I looked at a dozen or so paintings, especially the two winners, then left. I had my fill when I had gone that far. Next day, at 12:15, we were lucky to get a bus on the long 19 hour (believe it or not) trip home. Our fare cost, round trip, $27.86.

The *Crucifixion*, one of the medal and purchase winners is most crude and much left out. It also appears to me that the artist when painting this canvas had alongside of him Raphael's *Transfiguration*. If you will compare the two you'll readily see what I mean. Concept is along the same lines, also the composition: the hill where the crucifixion takes place—for pyramidal effect is easily comparable with Raphael's *Transfiguration*. Group in foreground is also comparable even to the little bit of expression on the faces, posture and etc. Surface technique is anything but vigorous, but he tried hard to get an effect comparable with the group in the *Transfiguration*.

60

In my opinion the drawing of forms is very poor indeed. Also it lacks much in what it takes to make up a painting—that is to measure up to those elements of power in art that are considered a standard.

The *Still Life* is a nice work but utterly ridiculous in the extreme. Some grass, a bottle, a pitcher, a bird's nest, some small tree limbs, done in mauve and green. My opinion of all stills is that they are nothing but kindergarten stuff. A grown man making a setting on a table or what have you and then painting it, is either too lazy to use his brain or he hasn't any brain. Stills, even the very best I would class as clever, cute or a time passer and incidentally a time waster. They all raved about the way the grass bent or bowed over in the Still, so what. Does this childish work give anything to the world? Does it make one think? Does it do anything? Just cute in my opinion. And, Ye Gods, they give a medal for it and purchased! It failed to emote me and I am very emotional. He hasn't gotten over his art class teachings. All the art schools are cluttered with stills and after they graduate they go out into the world and continue with their silly stills. In a more humorous vein, I prefer the moonshiners' still to the stills in art because the former at least stimulates.

I think my little excursion alone was worth the price I paid.

The canvas I'm working on now is *A Hunting He Would Go.*

P. S. The newspaper didn't even know I had a canvas entered. I wasn't even an "also ran"!

Sullivan has now given up house-painting, because its seasonal character does not permit him to make a living. Because of his age—he is 47—he had great difficulty in obtaining a new job. He was finally hired by a steel mill where he works so hard that he is too exhausted to paint pictures.

Sometimes I am too tired to eat or sleep. . . . I'd like to see an A. Lincoln or any other national hero work like I do all day and study law or anything else at night. . . . I haven't touched a canvas in months—my head is full of good pictures and I want to paint very very much.

Man's Procrastinating Pastime

THIS IS the painting to which Sullivan referred as his first "all original" and is the picture that I found in the Independent show, as related in the biographical note. Sullivan's theme is a comprehensive documentation of the artist's conception:

61

The forest is the sub-conscious mind of man. The trees are beech and chestnuts symbolical of the fruit the mind bears.

The man kneeling over the grave symbolizes mankind in general. He is burying the evil part of himself deep in the mind. (Man is always wasting time doing that.)

The tall formidable looking man is the good part of man urging him to get out of the deep mind—out into the conscious or clear light of day and perform good deeds and hide or bury his evil self that way. The good part of man has a club which symbolizes courage; the axe, will power and the knife, intellect. These three qualities are necessary, I think, for a successful life.

The grotesque creature to his right is my personification of sin. Sin is, or would be, just as silly or crazy looking, I think, if sin could be personified. The large head denotes the cunning of sin; the red sleeves are for passion; the black collar and pale tie for death and ruin; the cream waist for the apparent ease one has while in sin; the blue trousers for the allure of sin. The bony hands, jointless fingers and the large cumbersome feet are what I call paradoxical hands and feet. If one is willing, sin may easily catch up and hold with little or no trouble. However, if one is not willing, Sin with bony hands and jointless fingers and large pedal extremities couldn't catch up with a person in a thousand years of moons.

The large tree in the foreground, lying on the ground denotes something in the sin line that is a grievous offence and the smaller ones lying around denote venial offenses. The beech trees are pretty well on the road to a rotten condition (bad mind). Yet, as bad as they look, one of them has a branch hanging down (broken) still it is connected with the bark thus furnishing the life-giving sap to grow leaves and fruit of the limbs. (There's good in any broken life).

The three dark trees (chestnuts) bear no leaves or fruit as yet, but as soon as the man ceases delaying trying to bury or hide his evil self and perform some good deed these three strong sturdy trees will be there to bear the fruit of his good deeds.

Man is always procrastinating trying to hide his evil self instead of courageously showing his good part and performing good deeds—hence the title *Man's Procrastinating Pastime.*

Sullivan has given so clear and so detailed an account of the imagery, that we have an unusual opportunity to see from his own words how the composition developed and took form, how he transformed subject matter into symbols, and how these symbols entered into the construction of the painting. The eloquence with which he pleads his case in words is even more serious and strikingly intense when he delivers his sermon in paint.

The challenge of the figure of Sin, the morbid activity of the man burying his lesser self, the healthy command of the central figure, the overpowering density of the forest and the mystery of the symbolic earth: these are the forceful arguments with which he presents his convictions.

SULLIVAN *Man's Procrastinating Pastime.* 1936

These pictorial transcriptions, together with the infinite care and devotion he has given to the minutest detail, impart to the work a quality similar to that found in the early 15th century Italian masters.

He has created a labyrinth of contrasting branches and tree trunks which play in and out of the foliage across the upper half of the painting. Although the central figure obviously directs one's attention through the composition, there are other elements which work more subtly and tellingly to achieve this result. One first sweeps across the mound of earth in the foreground, at the end of which a series of small objects, pick, spade, shovel and sticks, point the general direction obliquely back into the picture. The line is boldly taken up by the fallen tree and the eye is led through the Gothic arch which opens up the heart of this archaic forest. Now delicate twigs which lie upon the earth catch the eye and guide it through the maze of tree trunks and ultimately into the light beyond.

Pictorially, the design is made more complex by the play of light and shadow which covers the entire surface of the picture. It patterns the rich brown earth in the foreground and the floor of the forest, and increases the impenetrability of the trees. It neutralizes the verdant forest colors, adding to the emotional impact by giving the forest a ghostly mien.

The color key which reflects Sullivan's vocational background is low and is confined to subtle tonalities of green greys and browns, relieved only by the figure of Sin which wears bright blue trousers and vivid red sleeves and belt. This is a functional idea necessary to his theme and marks a first departure from the color experiences of his vocation.

The pigment, heavily applied, increases by its sheer weight the force of Sullivan's thematic statement. It is built up in the figures, especially on the features of Sin, where it is used to intensify evil.

Of the central figure Sullivan writes:

I almost forgot to say something about the figure in *Man's Procrastinating Pastime* being a self-portrait. I really never had myself in mind but now as I look at it, it does resemble me somewhat in feature, contour and slender raw boned build. However, I didn't have myself in mind when I painted it. Probably subconsciously I may have worked myself into it.

In contrast to the decay which lies on the ground, the form of the freshly upturned earth which is piled across the front of the picture is a significant double image, for it resembles a reclining lion facing to the left, its head upon its paws, spreading itself along the picture frame. If we were to add the spear-shaped spade for its tail, it would cover the entire foreground. The eternal cycle of germination is subconsciously stated as Mother Earth becomes the father-image.

An Historical Event

In *An Historical Event*, which Sullivan painted in 1937, the romance of King Edward and Mrs. Wallis Simpson is depicted. This typical legendary romance of the king and the commoner has a new twist, in which the king gives up his crown. It is the kind of theme that has inspired a whole folk literature of song and story, and Sullivan's response shows that in this contemporary version it has lost none of its traditional appeal.

The accompanying theme, written by the artist, is an extension of the painting.

AN HISTORICAL EVENT

The picture as a whole is the heart of the ex-king. The blue sky and water denote love surging in his heart. The trees represent the many sturdy qualities and manly characteristics of the, or in the heart of the ex-king. The uniformity of the trees denote the harmony and exquisiteness of love. The fallen tree represents the pain and anguish (notwithstanding his great love for "Wally") in giving up, or abdicating, the throne a sort of upheaval in his heart. In the garden of this ex-king's heart is the lovely rose, the only flower in it and we see him busily engaged in tending to the growth of the rose (his love). He is removing twigs, stones and other debris from around the bush preparatory to hoeing around it. In the center foreground you will notice a bare ground spot. The way it is shaped will bring to your mind twins joined together as in the case of Siamese twins. "Wally" and Edward like the twins are inseparable—part them and it means the end of both.

65

On the right foreground of the canvas, as you know, is the British Lion and draped over his back is the national emblem of the British Empire and on top of that the crown. Cupid is ordering the lion and with it its empire representations out of the ex-king's heart. (He's telling him to "scram" with his trappings as he is of no use in the ex-king's heart.) Cupid's attitude is that of the victor over the vanquished. Having taken down the Lion's emblem and run up his own he is commanding as he stands pointing the way out, his left hand leaning on his bow and his kit of arrows lying on the ground beside him. There isn't a great difference between love and duty so the reason for the rocky road the lion is taking out. He must travel the road of duty carefully else the crown and emblem will fall from his back. The smooth part of the path, or road is the love road leading to the alluring blue love waters. Cupid's emblem, of course, depicts or denotes by the speared heart and the bow and arrow what his government is, or stands for—love.

P. S. I forgot to mention in the theme that the afternoon sun which the shadows indicate show that love came to Edward when his life was on the wane. He is 43 years of age. And "Wally"—well I'll bet she's close to Edward in age. Like the rose in the picture shows:—she is the big thing in his life.

Again we find the words of the artist most helpful in relating the thematic to the pictorial content. Consequently discussion here will be confined only to phases of the painting not touched upon in his written theme.

The painting divides itself into two unequal parts. The flagpole, as a manifestation of love through Freudian connotation, is a logical subconscious division. To the left are grouped the Edward figure, Wally as the flower, two trees which are upright and one that has fallen to the ground. The interest exerted here is equally as great as in the larger portion of the painting, which embraces the figure of Cupid, the lion and the crown, five of the trees, the road and the banner of love. Sullivan balances the simple fact of their love against the glamour of the throne.

This subtle way of creating balance—by the opposition of compensating factors—is a plastic idea variations upon which recur throughout the canvas.

Horizontals formed by the frontal plane, shore lines, tree tops and cloud formation, are countered by strong vertical rhythms, against which play the obliques of the uprooted tree, the shadow of the flagpole, the sticks, and of both insignia.

Although Sullivan uses cheerful color—green, red, yellow and light blue, the color mood is sombre. The trees are densely stippled with black, and the green grass is darkened with accents cast over it like iron filings. The disquieting oblique light of late afternoon only deepens the effect of the dark

66

SULLIVAN   *An Historical Event.* 1937

67

colors. Still this is a lyrical picture, although it is possibly the kind of lyricism one might expect to find engraved on Celtic rock.

Painting with painstaking devotion over a long period of time, Sullivan works the pigment into relief in many places. As a result a whole gamut of textures is achieved. To the smooth surfaces of the water are opposed the rougher surfaces of the bark and leaves of the trees; the deep ridges in the petals of the rose contrast with the raised modeling in the anatomy of the lion.

From the crown emanates a beatifying light, remembered from religious experience, and here glorifying kingly possessions. Conceptually, this holy light is unique in the picture, since it derives from a spiritual source, while all the other symbols have sources in mundane life and in folklore.

The trees, erect and each crowned with a busby of foliage, stand at attention like the Guards at Buckingham Palace.

Humorously enough, the face on the British Lion resembles Edward more closely than does the face on the Edward figure.

In the same spirit as *An Historical Event* is the Calypso, *Edward the VIII*, a Caribbean ballad sung to rhumba rhythms. The Calypso is a musical form which originated in Trinidad and is sung by the natives. It is usually based on current events, and is a spontaneous improvisation of words and music, a unique wedding of Negro and Latin-American music with Anglo-Saxon and Spanish speech.

Edward the VIII, sung by Rufus Callender (*The Caresser*) celebrates the famous King Edward-Wallis Simpson romance and converts it into legend with the same direct and simple spirit, with the warm sympathy for the participants and pleasure in the denouement that we find in Sullivan's *An Historical Event*. It was created in Trinidad in 1937 at the time that Sullivan was painting his picture in West Virginia.

Here are several of the verses and the chorus which weaves through them.

* Decca Recording #17298-A.

It's love it's love alone

That caused King Edward to leave the throne

Chorus: It's love it's love alone

That caused King Edward to leave the throne

We know Edward is noble and great
But love caused him to abdicate.

Repeat chorus.

Oh what a sad disappointment
Was endured by the British Government.

Repeat chorus.

On the 10th of December we heard the talk
That he gave the throne to the Duke of York.

Repeat chorus.

Am sorry my mother is going to grieve
But I cannot help I am bound to leave.

Repeat chorus.

They could take my throne they could take my crown
But leave me in Miss Simpson renown.

Repeat chorus.

No one in the annals of history
Has left a throne for his fancy free.

Repeat chorus.

69

The Fourth Dimension

FOR THE layman to grapple with the time-space concept is an undertaking of the first magnitude, but Sullivan does not hesitate. Heavenly-minded, he speculates with alacrity upon the domain of the heavens. If his solution is conditioned by a theological approach and is not arrived at solely through the laws of mathematics and physics, this is immaterial, since we are concerned here primarily with pictorial logic. And certainly in this he has achieved a remarkably personal solution. The theme explains his reasoning:

THE FOURTH DIMENSION

Man, a three dimensional creature is chained securely (figure standing) to a three dimensional planet. Man is ever trying to get beyond his three dimensional limit. He studies the multitudinous planetary system. He looks out into this infinite system of worlds and wonders, ponders on this and that: are the other planets peopled? Did our earth and the other planets appear in their particular position and operate by accident? Or did a powerful will create them?

Mathematicians and physicists have grappled with these and other unanswerable questions and the most intriguing of all is the question "What is the 4th dimension?" But with all his studying he is not able to comprehend or define it any more than he can square the circle. Man contemplates, studies this very intriguing question, but being a three dimensional creature chained to a three dimensional earth it is plain (to me at least) that he cannot go beyond his limit. A finite creature cannot delve into infinitude.

However, when death ensues, (figure lying) the chain holding man here is broken and his spirit (the spirit of a thing is the real thing) leaves the vehicle in which it toured this three-dimensional earth and is absorbed into Time from whence it came. The spirit then is not cognizant, or aware of any dimensions. It is infinite. The moment such a spirit's thought is of any particular part of the infinite vastness, it is immediately there. There are no dimensions, no limits. "End, there is none and there never was a beginning." So much for the subjective end.

It is, I think, impossible to show the 4th dimension objectively (or any way for that matter) but like many others I have tried. The planetary system I show isn't any particular setting. For lack of a name for the setting, I just call it Sullivan's universe. There are all kinds of planets in it: nebula, saturn-like planet, comet, stars, etc. Also I show the dark spots, called coal sacks by astronomers. The geometrical lines show height, width, length going out into infinity. The lines go thru' the hour glass which represents time. Tho' height, width and length go thru' time, time is with them. Time then is the 4th dimension. The hour glass is red to represent or show that all life has its being in time, (pulsating, vibrant, red life).

Compositionally this picture is unique. The surface of the earth forms

70

LLIVAN *The Fourth Dimension.* 1938

a convex plane which curves toward the observer. The heavens are so colored and drawn that, starting at the top of the canvas and returning toward the surface of the earth, they form a concave arc away from the observer. One gets the feeling that a cross-section of these two domes, one concave, the other convex, would make a huge S standing in deep space, were the picture not a canvas, but a three-dimensional object.

In *his* sky, Sullivan creates an illusion of deep space that curves. This he achieves with diminishing spherical forms which through subtle relationships follow curving recessions.

The galaxy of stars and planets makes the heavens vibrate. Differing in sizes, markings, weights and densities, they spin at varying rates of speed. Shooting and spiral movements intersperse the rotating spheres. Warm or cold lights illuminate each globe and those within the atmosphere of the earth may be seen to radiate beams of metaphysical starlight which spill strangely over the earth's surface.

The man standing in the path of this light casts a shadow which lies on the ground. The spirit, however, throws no shadow, but instead casts off the body which lies on the ground.

Lines of length and width pass through the hour-glass, forming a diagram which is placed on the earth like a cross. The third dimension, height, rises out of the hour-glass to join the only radiant star above the earth's atmosphere. Sullivan has here subconsciously converted a space concept into a Christian symbol involving the Cross, the Star of Bethlehem and the Holy Grail.

72

Haunts in the Totalitarian Woods

As SULLIVAN wrote in his "history," he destroyed the Ethiopia canvas in a rage after the fall of Ethiopia. *Haunts in the Totalitarian Woods* remains his only political picture. Finished early in February, 1939, it anticipated by 20 months the triple Axis pact.

At that time Sullivan wrote a very long letter as a preliminary to his theme, and an excerpt is quoted here:

. . . . Before I start on a canvas I see it with my mind's eye—that is the main or general idea or plan and as I go along I make a little change here a little change there a necessary invention here and there until finally it comes to life. Naturally there isn't anyone who can tell what my finished picture will be. By the way, do you like the title, *Haunts in the Totalitarian Woods?* This seemed better than just, *The Haunted Woods,* it is more dignified and in keeping with the canvas from a thematic viewpoint. The *Maginot Line* title would not do at all. Most people would wisecrack that civilization's maginot line is nothing but ghosts etc. I think the title I gave it hits it perfectly—don't you? One thing I'll say for the canvas, it sure is timely and, as the Chinese say, "it tells more than 10,000 words."

Sullivan later, as is his custom, sent the theme:

HAUNTS IN THE TOTALITARIAN WOODS

Hitler, Mussolini and Hirohito have been running rampant thru' the totalitarian woods of Europe and Asia. No one will deny that they are totalitarian Governments. The woods here represent those governments. They have arrived at the end of the (their) woods, as it were, and beyond it looks blackish and uncertain. Suddenly three spectres appear before them, awesome spectres attired in the authoritative colors of their respective governments. They look, they halt. They are fearful. These mad men want to pull their swords out, but they don't—they are really scared. They see paths to get to Britain and France. They see a hurdle (mound) to get over before they can get to the U. S. They fear to take the easy paths that seem to get to Britain and France because it seems to merge into the space behind the hurdle (mound) in front of the U. S.

73

On looking further they see that Britain, France and the U. S., Chamberlain, Dala-dier and Roosevelt seem to come out of the same cloud. In other words they see the three democracies coming out of their (cloud) source, the one thought or common spirit of all. Roosevelt seems to dominate, but all show a very aggressive, forbidding appearance. For the time, at least, these mad men have been halted. Thru' appeasement, it is true, but mostly thru' fear of the combined forces of democracy. The small mounds in the foreground represent the ulcers in the totalitarian woods—such as the rape of Czechoslovakia and Austria and the inhuman treatment and expulsion of the very people who built the German empire—the Jews. Also there is the rape of Ethiopia—a defenseless people. (I'd like to add here as an afterthought—Czechoslovakia and Ethiopia were isolationists yet we all know what happened to them. A lot of food for thought in this for advocates of isolationism—don't you think so?) Have you noticed that the three democracies all have the same colors in their national emblems—red, white and blue.

Sullivan's treatment of the woods is somewhat like that in *Man's Procrastinating Pastime*, except that here the color is heightened. The trees are covered with intense green foliage sharply shaded by blacks and the entire surface of the ground is bathed in a reddish glow which is reflected from the flaming spectres. Psychologically this is very effective since it suggests the heat of rising wrath. The sunlight which streaks from out of the halo of clouds over the Roosevelt head is introduced with exceptional pictorial effect. It acts as an additional tie for the three ghosts which are already joined together by the garlands of their respective flags. The red, white and blue color motif of the three flags is so interwoven as to solidify the three into a single integrated unit.

Mount Calvary, which Sullivan painted in an earlier picture called *Solitude,* is restated here in the spectres without conscious intent. The central figure, U. S. A., is sanctified with the religious halo. To the left, where tradition commands shall be the lost soul, is France, and to the right England, the one which may be saved. This political statement rendered by means of religious connotation, is interesting in the light of subsequent happenings, regardless of whether it was subconsciously or accidentally prophetic.

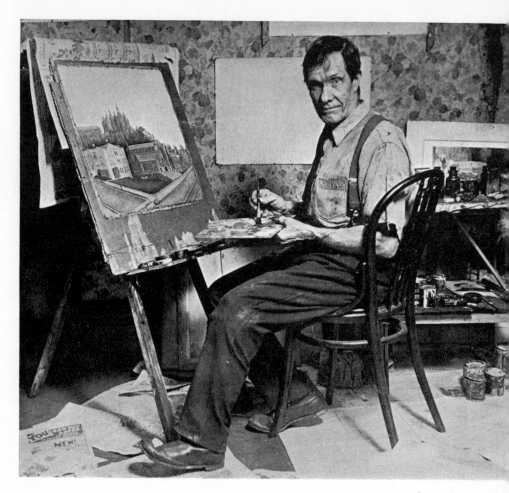

CHAPTER FIVE

JOHN KANE

ALWAYS returning to Pittsburgh as his home, John Kane expressed over and over again in his paintings the affection he had for this city. He felt the Whitmanesque epic of its industrial growth and expansion in a particularly personal way because he had worked on the actual construction of many of its buildings, bridges and streets.

Kane has said:

I have been asked why I am particularly interested in painting Pittsburgh. Her mills with their plumes of smoke, her high hills and deep valleys and winding rivers. Because I find beauty everywhere in Pittsburgh. The city is my own. I have worked on all parts of it, in building the blast furnaces and then in the mills and in paving the tracks that brought the first street cars out Fifth Avenue to Oakland. The filtration plant, the bridges that span the river, all these are my own. Why shouldn't I want to set them down when they are to some extent children of my labors? And when I see Pittsburgh I see it with my recollections as well as the way it now looks. And so I see it both the way God made it and as man changed it.

Born in 1860 in West Calder near Edinburgh, Scotland, of Irish parents, Kane was the third of a family of nine children. When he was ten years old, his father died, and John's first job was as a mine worker. He continued in the mines until he was nineteen, and then came to America on a boat that took eighteen days to cross from Glasgow. Settling in Pittsburgh, he traveled about the country on various jobs. His many occupations invariably required manual labor, but his strong body thrived under it, and he reveled in his strength.

In 1897, Kane had married Maggie Halloran, "as pretty a lass as ever come out of Ireland, or England, or any other country the world around." Their first two children were girls. The third, a boy, died the day after birth, and this was such a blow to Kane that it marked a turning point in his life. He lost interest in work and in his responsibilities as head of the family, which eventually caused intermittent family estrangements over a period of twenty-five years.

Kane always liked to draw, and as early as 1890 made pencil sketches of scenes that interested him. On three different occasions he tried to go to art school, once in Pittsburgh when the Carnegie Institute opened a fine-arts course, another time in Charleston, W. Va., and a third in Cleveland. Each attempt failed, chiefly because he had no money to pay for lessons. Kane said in this connection:

But I was not put out to any extent when all three of these attempts failed, for I believe generally God finds a way to help those inclined to art. And so it was in my case.

He was also unsuccessful in an effort to get a job as helper to John W. Alexander, an academician, who was then doing a series of murals for the Carnegie Institute.

His first experience in the use of color came at the turn of the century when he got a job as a painter of freight cars, and later he colored photo-enlargements. Subsequently he was a house-painter and called this his "out-door painting," as contrasted with his painting oils on canvas which he termed his "pictorial work." Of these three occupations which led finally to his painting pictures, the practice acquired in coloring photographs was to cause unpleasant publicity at his first one-man showing at the Junior League, Pittsburgh, in 1931.

At this time two local newspapers bought paintings out of the exhibition and by arrangement removed the paint from half of each picture to expose a photograph beneath. Both had been painted over photographs which particularly appealed to Kane as a father. Of these he said:

One was called *Dad's Pay Day*. It showed two little girls and a little lad waiting at the steps of their home for their father to come with his wages. Now the little girls reminded me of Mary and Margie when they were small, and the boy was how I fancied our John would look if he lived to be a tot of two or three. It appealed to me for that was the way our little girls used to wait for me to give them pennies.

The other was called *The Doctor*. A little lad was playing he was the doctor. In his hand was a watch. He was counting the pulse beats of a sick dolly.

Kane had not the remotest idea that he had done something which might be criticized as unethical. He had colored photographs commercially, and on a few he had innocently gone further and painted over them entirely. His response to the action of the newspapers in running these pictures was:

It is my observation that he who destroys a thing another has labored to create murders a dead man.

All of the foregoing quotes have been gleaned from the American classic *Sky Hooks,* the autobiography of Kane as told to Marie McSwigan, who met him in 1927 just as he was about to emerge from obscurity. At this time, Miss McSwigan, a reporter on *The Pittsburgh Press*, learned that a house painter who lived in the Strip, Pittsburgh's worst slum, was to "crash" the Carnegie Institute, and she was assigned to cover the story. Over a period of years she was to see Kane regularly, as he was constantly in the news.

Kane, like many self-taught artists, had turned to his local museum for recognition. In 1924 and 1925 he climbed the stairs of the Carnegie Institute with a painting under his arm, and each time, Director Homer St. Gaudens was obliged to reject the entry because it was a copy. Later, Kane learned that there were formalities involved in submitting pictures, and in 1926, John O'Connor, Jr. of the Institute informs me, Kane sent four paintings, none of them copies, but none was accepted by the jury. However, in 1927, his *Scene from the Scottish Highlands* passed the Carnegie jury largely through the efforts of the artist, Andrew Dasburg, a juror. The next seven years, until his death from tuberculosis, in August, 1934, brought constantly increasing recognition.

In the introductory comment on *Sky Hooks*, Frank Crowninshield writes:

Few careers in the long history of art have been more singular than that of John Kane. Everything in it seems to have come from the other side of probability. Search Vasari's *Lives of the Artists* from beginning to end, and you will find in them no more magnificent paradox than this: that an immigrant day-laborer, who had no time to paint, no money to paint, no earthly provocation or encouragement to paint, should yet emerge, at the age of sixty-seven, as the most significant painter America has produced during the past quarter-century.

Sky Hooks is Kane's story, just as it fell from his lips during the last two years of his life. . . . John Kane was among other things a house-painter. He was also a miner, a steel-worker, a street-paver, a watchman at a railroad crossing, a construction-gang foreman, a munitions worker, a master carpenter, and a fist-fighter of some renown. He used to say, "I have done almost every kind of work a laboring man can do." . . . It is fortunate for his memory and for the public at large that he should have found, before his death, a friend so sympathetic, an admirer so sincere, and an amanuensis so faithful as Marie McSwigan. . . .

. . . She noted the incidents of his checkered life in his own words; . . . they have resulted in a human document which possesses the charm, the dignity, the impressiveness of complete simplicity; a portrait, life size, of a heroic and, somehow, Biblical figure.

The following excerpts from this book throw light on his "pictorial work":

It was at McKees Rocks early in the century that I began painting steel cars, and in this way I learned the use of paint. At once I saw the possibility of coloring my scenes and pictures. I had always loved to draw. I now became in love with paint. For now I could color the sketches I had made with pencil. At noon I would slip into the yard while others were eating their lunches. I would draw a scene on the side of a box car and would color it. Oh, it was glorious. It was the first opportunity I ever had

79

of making the pictures that were in my mind in the beauty and wide range of colors that nature had given them.

The best thing in the world for a young artist would be to hire himself out to a good painting contractor who knows his business. Of that I am convinced. I believe that many a young art student would profit greatly in his work if he learned to paint as an outdoor painter does, rather than confine his painting entirely to art school.

I preferred to paint. But if there was no painting to be done, I could fall back on my full-fledged carpenter's card to show. I was never sorry I learned this work. Like outdoor painting, it helped me with my art.

In another way this knowledge of carpentry has helped me with my art work. Now that I am exhibiting oil paintings I sometimes like to make the frames myself. In that way I can get them suitable in every respect. I like to size the wood, to mortice and join the edges and cover them with gold-leaf. I also make crates and packing cases to send my pictures to exhibitions. All this comes handy for a man to know.

For in the art of painting, there is the art of mixing colors. I get myself the three primary colors, red, blue and yellow, and I use black and white to lighten or darken my color schemes as the need arises. In that way I can get any shade under the sun.

I take pains with my work. . . . I think a painting has a right to be as exact as a joist or mould or any other part of building construction. I think the artist owes it to the people to make his painting as right and as sound as he can make it.

And it may be that the old masters, too, like myself, found nothing too humble for their brushes. They made angels out of the children of the Italian streets by putting wings on them. Thus they increased the idea of innocence the children meant to them.

Kane has left behind a host of friends, and one, particularly close to him, apparently the only person to have seen him paint, is Alex Fletcher, Greensburg, Pa., house-painter, a self-taught artist himself. He has written me the following reminiscences of their friendship:

I got to know John Kane in 1927. As I looked at him I felt in my bones that must be John Kane. I walked over and said Are you John Kane. He said Yes. I said I knew it, but don't know why. My name is Alex Fletcher, Scotchman from Greensburg. Mighty glad to meet you. I landed in New York April 18, 1888—and I told him my age. I was drawn to him right there and then. He looked up at me and said Well, Alex Fletcher, I beat you two ways. I am a good five years older than you and I was here a good five years before you. We both laughed. . . .

At first he could not dispose of his pictures for a price that would enable him to keep house and get Mrs. Kane back to Pittsburgh. He lived in one room in the Strip—it was a sleeping room, living room, studio, dining room, all combined, pictures stacked up on one side and bed in the middle, stove, bureau, two chairs and paint material took up the other side. . . .

John did not like to have people look at him painting. However he sometimes painted before me. I do not know what system he had in drawing because I was never there when he laid out a picture, but I do know he took a long time to make a picture.

80

He used slow drying color, and much oil,—the color thin. He coated in the sky, blue-white and the clouds white, but not the cloud shadows yet. Now when dry he is ready to shade or glaze down with thin deeper color over the whole picture. All John's pictures are glazed, perhaps the landscapes more so than the pictures with buildings and bridges, and this took much more time in glaze over detail and pencil work than he got credit for. . . .

John was not doing good and was so proud and independent you could not do anything for him. He would resent it. . . .

As sure as you live Alex, John said, I was going to move out to Oakland, Ophelia St., but this street car accident happened and I dont know if they will keep the little apartment for me, and Mrs. Kane is back. I knew John needed money, but how to get him to take it I did not know. I liked his pictures and liked him so I said, John, I want you to paint a picture for me. Oh sure Alex, I will, and it won't cost you anything. I said The heck, John, I dont want it if it dont cost anything. I said I have two pictures of Walters I paid him $60 each for size 16x20, so you paint me one. Not now, but whenever you're fit. I put $20 down on the table for he would not take it. I said first payment. Then he said, what kind of picture do you want. I said any kind. I like them all. Small picture, and put your name on the corner.

Just then Mrs. Kane came in with a bottle of milk. John said, I was painting my wife and I could not get her. I looked at Mrs. Kane and I said to John, When you are painting the picture for me, dont forget, I dont want your wife. I have one. She said in her delightful Irish accent, One wife is enough. If you have more than one that is the start of all your troubles.

About two weeks after this I thought now John will be out of money and so I sent $20. more, later I sent the third $20. In a few days I got a letter from John Kane with a P.O. money order for what I sent him. The letter said, Alex I am all right now. I sold three pictures and got $750 for the three, one to Mrs. Rockefeller, one to Dewey (I forget the third one). You see, John still thought I was buying the picture to help him out. I took the money order and endorsed it over and wrote, Now, John, you crazy duck, I still want the picture and like your pictures and get that notion out of your head that I was buying the picture to help you out. I will get that picture when I get to see our show in March. I still treasure this painting.

EARLY COLLECTORS OF JOHN KANE'S WORK

Before his official recognition in 1927, Kane painted two or three pictures of farmhouses, and these were purchased by the owners of the farms he painted. He had also given paintings as gifts, for example, the portraits of Bishop Boyle and Father Cox, which he presented to the Sisters at St. Patrick's School.

The following list begins with the first painting purchased, and includes many of his works acquired up to the time of the first one-man show, 1931, in New York. Some of these paintings have since changed hands.

YEAR ACQUIRED	COLLECTOR	TITLE
1927	Andrew Dasburg, New York	*Scene from the Scottish Highlands*
1928	Edward Duff Balkan, Pittsburgh	*Squirrel Hill Farm*
1929	John Dewey, New York	*Coleman Hollow* (small version)
1929	Leon Kroll, New York	*End of the Day*
1930	Edward Frohman	One Oil
1930	Chas. Ward Friend	*Old Clinton Furnace*
1930	Father Cox, Pittsburgh	*Portrait of Father Cox*

"Father Cox, the pastor of St. Patrick's Church, was the one who led the jobless army to Washington during Hoover's administration, and who also ran for President of the United States on the Jobless Ticket."— *Sky Hooks.*

| 1930 | Dr. H. H. Permar, Pittsburgh | *Portrait of Bishop Boyle* |

Given to Dr. Permar by Father Cox.

| 1930 | Phillips Memorial Gallery, Washington | *Across the Strip* |

First Museum to acquire a Kane painting

1930	Mrs. Maximilian Elser	*Along the Susquehanna*
1930	Marie McSwigan, Pittsburgh	*Mt. Mercy*
1930	Mrs. John D. Rockefeller, Jr., New York	*Homestead*
1931	Alex Fletcher, Greensburg, Pa.	*Steel Farm*

See Fletcher's letter describing the transaction, above.

1931	Burton Emmett, New York	*Nine Mile Run*
1931	Bartlett Arkell, New York	*Along the Susquehanna* (small version)
1931	*The Sun Telegraph*, Pittsburgh	*The Doctor**
1931	*The Pittsburgh Press*, Pittsburgh	*Dad's Payday**

MAJOR EXHIBITIONS IN WHICH KANE PARTICIPATED,
1927-1941

YEAR	EXHIBITION	PAINTINGS
1927	Carnegie International, Pittsburgh	*Scene from the Scottish Highlands*
1928	Carnegie International, Pittsburgh	*Old Clinton Furnace*
1928	Associated Artists, 18th Annual, Pittsburgh	Six Oils
		Turtle Creek Valley: 2nd Prize, $100.

* See p. 78.

YEAR	EXHIBITION	PAINTINGS
1929	Carnegie International, Pittsburgh	*Homestead*
1929	Associated Artists, 19th Annual, Pittsburgh	Five Oils
1929	Harvard Society of Contemporary Art, Cambridge	Five Oils
		Nude *Self-Portrait* rejected*
1930	Toledo Museum of Art, Toledo	*Homestead*
1930	Harvard Society of Contemporary Art, Cambridge	Five Oils
1930	Associated Artists, 20th Annual	Two Oils
1930	Museum of Modern Art, New York, "Living Americans"	Three Oils
1931	Junior League, Pittsburgh	Thirty Oils—
	First one-man show	
1931	Contemporary Art Galleries, East 10th Street, New York	Twenty Oils
	First one-man show in New York, recommended by Patrick Codyre	
1931	Carnegie International	*Monongahela Valley*
1932	Exhibition of Pittsburgh Painters	*From my Studio Window*†
1932	Associated Artists, 21st Annual	Two Oils
1932	Gallery 144—13th St., New York	Twenty Oils
1932	Pennsylvania Academy of Fine Arts, Philadelphia, 127th Annual	Two Oils
1932	Addison Gallery of American Art, Andover, Mass.	*Old Elm*
1932	Whitney Museum, New York, 1st Biennial	*Turtle Creek Valley*
		Four Oils
1933	Associated Artists, 22nd Annual	*Liberty Bridge*—1st Prize $150
1933	Carnegie International	*Industry's Increase*†
1933	Pennsylvania Academy of Fine Arts, Philadelphia, 128th Annual	*My Thrift Garden*
1934	College Art Association, Circulating Exhibition	*Touching Up*†
1934	Carnegie International	*Crossing the Junction*
		Kane's last painting— unfinished
1934	Associated Artists, 23rd Annual	Two Oils
1934	Whitney Museum, 2nd Biennial	*Scots Day at Kennywood*
1934	Museum of Modern Art, Fifth Anniversary Show	*Scots Day at Kennywood*
1934	Pennsylvania Academy of Fine Arts, 129th Annual	*Penn Township*

* Kane later painted over this full length nude, a portrait, *Brother Patrick,* as a private in the Black Watch.
† Reproduced.

83

YEAR	EXHIBITION	PAINTINGS
1935	Valentine Gallery, New York 1st Memorial Retrospective	Twenty-eight Oils
1935	Chicago Arts Club, Chicago "Sidney Janis Collection"	*Through Coleman Hollow*
1936	Carnegie International-Memorial Retrospective	Forty-six Oils
1936	Albright Art Gallery, "Art of Today"	*Through Coleman Hollow*
1936	Knoedler & Co., London First one-man show abroad	Thirty-five Oils
1937	Valentine Gallery	Nineteen Oils
1938	U.S. Dept. of Labor Bldg., Washington, D.C.—Memorial Show	Fifteen Oils
1938	Museum of Modern Art— "Masters of Popular Painting"	Twenty Oils
1938	Wildenstein's, London	Thirty Oils
1939	Chicago Arts Club	Twenty-five Oils
1940	Addison Gallery of American Art	*Through Coleman Hollow*
1941	American Art for South American Re- publics	Two Oils
1941	Valentine Gallery—"Four Americans"	Two Oils

DUPLICATION OF TITLES IN KANE'S WORK

Kane painted two or more versions of several of his pictures, but never of the same size and often with slight changes or minor variations. In this category are notably:

Escape
Turtle Creek Valley
Mount Mercy
Mount Academy
Along the Susquehanna
Coleman Hollow
Nine Mile Run

Monongahela Valley
Lincoln's Gettysburg Address
Panther Hollow
Steel Farm
Juniata River
*Scots Day at Kennywood**

---

* There are at least three paintings by this name and all of them are compositionally different.

From My Studio Window

IN ORDER to make a comparison between actual scene and painting, I went to Pittsburgh to have photographs made of specific places which John Kane painted. In researching on the painting *From My Studio Window*, I found that Kane's home at 1700 Fifth Avenue, a corner building, had been demolished. Consequently, photos had to be taken from a corresponding apartment in the same type of building next door. Kane had lived on the second floor, with his studio on the third. The photographic shot reproduced here was oriented to the small church spire that protrudes above the second building from the right, as it does in the painting.

From the front window of the apartment, it was impossible to include the large office buildings in the background, as they were not visible at this point. While the angle from the side window allowed for but two of the background buildings, still it included more detail than any other point of view. It was from this window that the photograph finally was taken.

In looking for the rest of the buildings included in the Kane painting, I found it necessary to go to a higher floor from which I could get the additional view of the remaining buildings both on the street and in the background, but in focusing on this latter group, there was no longer a view of the right-hand half of the picture. In order to get in all the buildings Kane had compressed into his painting, it would have been necessary to take a panorama shot, and from two levels, at that.*

---

* "It would only be common sense to look at my scenes and to see that no camera was ever constructed to get the view of objects that I, as artist, see in paint. I don't believe anyone in his right mind would credit a camera with such faculties."—*Sky Hooks*

Photograph of the actual scene: *From My Studio Window*.

86

NE *From My Studio Window.* 1932.   Collection Miss Adelaide Milton de Groot.

87

Therefore "From My Studio *Windows*" would more accurately title the painting, for Kane undoubtedly painted this scene not only from his front windows on the second and third floor, but from the side windows as well. Thus he gave us a composite view, which, regardless of the fact that the view from his studio window was in recession, he placed upon a horizontal plane.

In doing this, he has invented, in a subtle and creative way, a form of diminishing perspective, for the windows are widest at the extreme right and narrow almost imperceptibly until they become mere slits on the buildings at the extreme left. Although the street-car tracks and the curb-line parallel the bottom of the frame, the gradual narrowing of the buildings and particularly of the window slits along the block suggest recession. Kane has given perspective, not by rules, but by reason of his own visual findings.

Although the painter stood as close to the street as the camera did, still in the foreground of his painting the traffic and houses are reduced in scale in relation to the actual scene, while office buildings in the background are enlarged. We find then that not only did he compress his composition laterally, but in depth as well.

The architecture is not composed of blocks of buildings nor phantom facades. Each is given its own personality, its own identity. In color and form each has its distinct aspect. Most striking is the absence of the deep green of nature, the color above all others associated with Kane's work. Neither are his heavy billowing clouds here, and his buildings in pinks and rusts, reds and browns are set within the borders of pale sky blue and pavement greys. The vehicles and figures in the foreground are gay color notes interspersed throughout the neutrals of the street.

Through the eight years that elapsed between the painting of this picture and the taking of the photograph, only one store tenant remained, Samuel Levin, tailor, at #1627, and his name may be seen above his awning both in the photograph and the painting.

Kane, for all the seriousness of his painting, did not lack the humor to include his friends and acquaintances as models. Here he placed them on wagons and trucks, in the street, and in *Industry's Increase*, we will find others as flagmen and engineers.

88

Touching Up

KANE PAINTED two versions of *Lincoln's Gettysburg Address*, and the one that appears on the easel in *Touching Up* is the larger version.

In this connection, Kane is quoted as saying in *Sky Hooks*:

I started an oil painting I have with me today. It is the oldest of my works that I know about, the oldest that exists for a certainty today. It is Lincoln's Gettysburg Address, word for word and letter for letter against an American flag as a background. In one corner I painted Lincoln's head. On the reverse, the back of the canvas, I made a very small portrait of Washington with the words, "Let us raise a standard to which all men can repair. The event is in the hand of God."

Now Washington's words were packed with wisdom. They were honest, simple and direct. But Lincoln's words, I have always considered, contained thoughts among the most beautiful ever expressed in speech or writing. His address is, to my mind, among the greatest works of great men. Abraham Lincoln has always been a hero to me. He was a father and a man of mercy from beginning to end. No widow or orphan ever went to him with a request that was refused.

I believe he was a healthy robust young fellow like myself, in his young days and mine. He started life as I did, without anything except what he got for himself. He had no schooling but what he worked for. And so I have always thought he was pretty much like myself, strong of body, willing to work and without the advantages that have helped other men.

Now Abraham Lincoln has a message for the artist as well as for everyone else. Nothing is denied to well-directed labor. Nothing is obtained without it. And that, Abraham Lincoln always stood for.

Each February this double painting would be called upon to perform a ritual, and the two parades that passed along Pittsburgh's Fifth Avenue during the month, were greeted from Kane's window by a painting appropriate to the occasion.

In *Touching Up*, a rapport is immediately felt to exist between the portrait on the easel and the Kane portrait which faces it, and the tension between them is increased by the presence of the chair which occupies the

89

center of the stage and is placed midway between them. It is as if this homely and humble object were a common bond.

On the painting of Lincoln are his timeless words, so respectfully recorded that every word is legible, and strung along the walls is a series of pictures, each a faithful recording of the original which hung in the room—the "timeless words" of John Kane. So that they too may be clearly seen, Kane has placed them high up next to the ceiling, and even he, who was six feet tall, does not cover any part of them.

Kane has so dedicated himself to *Touching Up* that he has made of it a series of portraits, of himself and of those things which tie up with his special loves: first and foremost the Lincoln painting, then on the walls, his family, scenes of Pittsburgh, memories of Scotland, and religion—all are portraits. Finally there is the little corner of the room which his wife called "John's glory hole," with its sparse furniture and make-shift painting paraphernalia.

His home-made easel consists of a wooden tripod, two of the legs bored with a series of holes in which are placed movable pegs to support the canvas at any given height. Partly obscured by the easel is a work-dresser, carefully grained to simulate the imitation graining with which Kane had more than likely decorated the original. It is also adorned with the usual gilt handles. His paint supplies may be seen atop it and paint cloths are protruding from the lower drawer. On the wall will be recognized the same design of wallpaper that appears in *My Grandson*.

In the painting, Kane, who has left his chair for a moment to get a better view of the canvas on the easel, is dressed in his customary painting garb which he "wore to the end of his painting days because he knew where to find everything in the pockets." Attached to the overalls are implements of his "outdoor painting," a large housepaint brush slipped through a back loop and a putty knife lodged in a side pocket.

In this carefully painted profile portrait, Kane has included his palette and brush, and so accurate is he in his biographical statement that on the palette may be seen all the colors he used in the painting on the easel, and the color on the tip of his brush suggests the part of the picture on which he was working at this point in the process of touching up.

90

NE   *Touching Up.* 1932

Industry's Increase

IN COMPARING the painting *Industry's Increase* with a photograph of the actual scene, we are struck at once by the fact that Kane has dramatized the values, achieving a fanciful and vibrant rendering of commonplace facts, and altering the whole character of the scene. The feeling of industrial growth and community development is extracted like precious metal from ore, and presented with the warmth of sympathetic interpretation.

Kane, in transposing nature to suit his pictorial needs, has narrowed the span of the bridge in order to bring the other shore within easy seeing distance. This enabled him to portray in clear detail the industrial activity and the homes which pepper the hills.

In the photograph the lower half is given over to a wide expanse of railroad yard, out of all proportion to its pictorial interest. Kane, in painting, has narrowed this into a small triangle which he has packed with interest by making every part work actively within a confined area. To accomplish this, it was necessary to shorten the distance between the bridge tower and the curve at the bridge approach to one-third its actual length.

All the details in the foreground including the street,* the river traffic and the bridge itself were sketched from the approximate point where the photograph was taken; the opposite shore and background obviously were not. Kane moved his position to more than half way across the bridge and from this vantage point recorded in careful detail the rolling hills which loomed up before him in full view. Even from here, the hills have been enlarged, giving them a more telling character.

In the photograph the smoke has caused a haze to obscure details of the background. Smoke pours from the chimneys in the painting too, but the atmosphere remains surprisingly clear. Visually Kane was able to penetrate the smoke-screen, where the filter of the camera failed.

In the actual scene there is little pictorial organization, but Kane enables

* "I paved along Carson Street (1890), the very street I painted in *Industry's Increase* for the Carnegie Institute International Exhibition of Paintings. I never thought in those days that I would show in an art exhibit a picture of the street I paved. But even at that time I had my pencil in my hand."—*Sky Hooks*.

one to traverse a continuous path throughout the painting. Paralleling the train which cuts into the composition at the bottom, one enters the spearhead of the picture via the street and rounds the curve approaching the bridge. Crossing obliquely to the other side, the observer's path steps up along a series of buildings to reach the lowest of the thin white roads, which enters the picture at the left. From here he travels a whimsical course along the white roads which mark the landscape. These cross the picture back and forth, constantly ascending, and finally bring one to rest upon the hilltops, so thickly covered with houses, in the distance.

The rising and falling curved lines of the suspended bridge cables are repeated in variations in the hilltops, and these become a kind of suspension bridge from which the roads, like cables, are strung with rows of little houses. The clouds in a series of arches directly above the hills, follow their general contour, and along the ceiling of the painting, Kane's characteristically heavy clouds float above the scene despite their volume.

To Kane, tremendous detail was no obstacle. On the contrary, he has said of it: "There it was daring me to paint it." In *Industry's Increase*, not only is everything fully controlled but it is integrated into a design as compact as it is intricate. Streets, tracks, trains, figures, the boats, the bridge and factories, everything, including the well-settled hills, is touched with the love and understanding that can come only from an artist whose mind is keenly charged with knowledge of his subject. Kane himself was a builder, and his compositions are soundly constructed. Of this he told his biographer:

It has been said that I am able to apply technical knowledge to my industrial scenes, my paintings of steel mills, furnaces, pipe factories, and of buildings and bridges of all sorts. Another man might paint a plant that could never stand up, but not I. I know how that building is erected for I have worked on every part of it from digging the foundations to the entire structure. Floor by floor I know how it goes up. I can see where the foundations come in and I take that into account when I am painting the surrounding details. If I paint a building, you may be sure it sits square on solid foundations and is built according to the laws of construction which take into consideration the laws of nature and gravity.

And who can deny that the patient laying of brick upon brick to get the whole, the intimate knowledge of all the parts and their relation to each other, has been carried over into his paintings, not only in the construction of the buildings, but also in the patient laying of detail upon detail to obtain

93

Photograph of the actual scene: *Industry's Increase.*

94

NE *Industry's Increase.* 1933.   Collection William S. Paley.

his own distinctive, tremendously varied patterns, and to coordinate and unify them pictorially?

Errors in spelling often appear in Kane's work, especially when, next to his signature, he lettered the title of the painting. Here one of the factory signs, *Byers Pipe*, is painted *Byers Pips*, a colloquial recommendation perhaps of Byers' superior quality.

Light and dark patterns vibrate throughout the picture. White clouds, the spotting of houses and the diffused light on the distant hills, the smoke and steam puffing from the factory chimneys as well as from the trains and river vessels, add to the industrial medley. The water cascading over the stern-wheeler picks up this vibration and leaves in its wake a herringbone pattern which becomes the backbone of the river.

My Grandson

JOHN KANE depicts his grandson in the act of drawing a picture of "Gram" on a school slate. The painting, besides being a portrait of the child, Lawrence Corbett, is a double recording of Mrs. Kane, one being on the slate, the other a photograph precariously perched on the dresser top.

Kane has caught the real feeling of intimacy of the child's world. The child is placed near the floor—his natural locale. Seated on a footstool between the dressers, he has found a comfortable little nook for himself. In scale he is larger than the furniture about him, because he was the most important focus for the artist. But contrary to expectation, this does not make him look out of proportion. Somehow it adjusts the environment more satisfactorily to the sphere of the child, and the dressers become toy furniture. Cutting off the composition across the top is Kane's way of excluding the adult world, and cutting it off at the side further protects the child from possible intrusion.

The pot of Easter lilies on the dresser is doubled by its reflection in the mirror against which it stands. A further reminder of the season is given in the small picture of the Madonna and Child which is peering out of the disheveled dresser drawer.

There is another reflection in the mirror, that of a window which is oppo-

96

NE *My Grandson.* 1930

site. One of the first things one notices in this picture is a light shining directly on the boy, which seems unusually strong for an interior, but now we have the clue, for sunlight is streaming in from this window and the boy sits directly in its path.

Kane's handling of this light and shade and the shadows is extremely knowing. Unlike most self-taught artists, he has neither eliminated nor ignored shadows, but on the contrary is keenly aware of them, and has integrated them as forms in his composition. The gradations of light and shade across the linoleum floor and the shadows on the wallpaper reveal both understanding and control. While the meticulous patternings undergo color changes in passing from light to dark areas, the design of each remains intact. These sensitive color changes add to the mood of the picture by breaking up the monotony of the pattern without sacrificing any of its effectiveness.

As a matter of fact the painting is a combination of many patterns, creating complex linear and color rhythms that are subtly contrasted and pictorially integrated. The curly head of golden hair on the child and the curlicues of grey on the black footstool; the curving folds shadowed on the boy's light grey suit; the waves of graining in the dressers, one golden oak, the other light oak; the small diamonds and fleur-de-lis in the light blue wallpaper together with larger buff-and-gold blocks in the linoleum: these designs enclose the child and create for him, in a sense, the pattern of his environment.

The surface of the canvas is covered with gritty pigment heavily applied, giving to the picture a homespun quality in keeping with its subject matter.

To emulate the brass handles and the edge of the Bible on the dresser, Kane used gilt. Many self-taught artists use metal paint to obtain verisimilitude, and Kane did this often. In painting a locket worn by his younger daughter in one picture, and a brass bird cage in another, he used gilt to signify metal. There are many other examples of this practise in his work. Expert at mixing oil paints, he could readily have done so in order to get a proper result, but evidently preferred the more direct means and the effect obtained thereby. His occupational past undoubtedly contributed to this practise, but ecclesiastical associations may also have had their importance, for Kane was a religious man and saw many reproductions of illuminated manuscripts and religious paintings, to which he responded keenly.

98

BLACKSMITH-SCULPTOR OF CHAGRIN FALLS AND HIS TOMBSTONE.

CHURCH.

Henry Church, the eccentric resi- | For a long time it stood in his front | neck, completes the group. Mr
at of Chagrin Falls, who died Fri- | yard. Later it was removed to the | Church's idea was to combine the
r, and the monument which he | cemetery. It represents a lion, near | Scriptural passage relating to the
ved out of a solid block of sand- | which a lamb rests contentedly, | lion and lamb lying down together
tone several years before his death. | while a little child, holding a chain | with that of "a little child shall lead
| which is tied around the animal's | them."

CHAPTER SIX

HENRY CHURCH

SINCE HIS discovery of the work of Henry Church, Sam Rosenberg, a New York writer, photographer, artist, and stage manager, has made a research of the history of Chagrin Falls, Ohio, back to the time of the pioneers, and has very carefully collected all data pertaining to the life of Church and his ancestors. The following account is a condensation of the material and includes but a few highlights in the colorful career of Church, blacksmith, painter, sculptor, musician, spiritualist, preacher.

99

HENRY CHURCH OF CHAGRIN

By Sam Rosenberg

In 1937 I drove out to see Squaw Rock, a landmark in Northern Ohio. A friend had told me that this high-relief sculpture was commonly believed to have been carved by prehistoric Indians. I contended that the Indians of Ohio had never done any such sculpture and promptly went out with my friend, Arthur Feher, to investigate the legend.

We soon came to the Squaw Rock Picnic Ground (about twelve miles from Cleveland) where signs told us that we would have to walk. We followed the dark trails leading downward into the deep ravine cut by the Chagrin River and suddenly, through the leafless trees and the early Spring mist, we saw the massive fallen cliff called Squaw Rock.

All we could see as we hastened towards it, was the life-sized figure of an Indian Woman surrounded by an enormous snake.

But a moment later, standing in front of it, we were able to see the other objects carved on the rock. They were, without any apparent connection to each other: a child in its crib, a mountain lion hanging by its tail, a tomahawk, a skeleton, and a spread eagle which might have been swooping down to rescue the Indian Woman from the serpent.

Finally, Arthur spoke: "What do you think?"

"This certainly isn't Indian." I said. "It's the work of some backwoods Rousseau. Whoever made this must have carved other things like it. Let's go look for him. Say, who do you suppose it was?"

Arthur pointed to one of the names carved on the rock. "What about that one?" he said. "The name HENRY CHURCH 1885. He might have done it. But maybe he just carved his name on the rock like the others."

We talked to several park workers. None of them knew anything about Squaw Rock, so we set out to get information in Chagrin Falls, the nearest town.

We mapped out our strategy on the highway to Chagrin. I was to question the first old resident we could find. We sped into town and cruised until we passed what looked like the oldest inhabitant.

The old man grinned at all my questions and said: "Squaw Rock was carved by a man who lived right here in Chagrin. Anybody here could have told you about him. He was a blacksmith by the name of Henry Church. There's all kinds of stories about him, some true and some false. Some say he carved the Squaw by the light of a lantern. On one side he had the Indian girl and the serpent, and on the thirty foot side, which you can only see from the other side of the river, he began the life story of Abe Lincoln, from Log Cabin to White House. The squaw used to be *painted* and was a *treat* to see."

The old man still grinned at us. "That ain't all, though," he said. "Old Hank also carved out his own tombstone and then he preached his own funeral sermon on a gramophone cylinder. He's dead about thirty years now and you'll find him and his tombstone, in the town cemetery, a mile down that road."

We made that mile in about sixty seconds.

URCH *The Rape of the Indian Tribes by the White Man.* (Rock Carving)

The cemetery of Chagrin is a conventional little park, filled with conventional granite stones and landscaped with properly mournful evergreens.

But, on a small northern slope, we were startled by an archaic, angry lion with green glass eyes. It was Henry Church's tombstone.

It was now quite dark. Arthur and I sat on the grass near the great, archaic lion and talked about the strange talent of this blacksmith and we tried to guess at the meanings behind the cryptic sculpture we had seen.

Several days later we returned to Chagrin armed with a long list of questions, ready to interview all the residents of the little town, if need be: we were determined to find out all there was to know about Henry Church.

Most of our questions were very ably answered by Mrs. Jessie Sargent, Church's daughter. This keen woman, now in her late seventies, liked talking about her father. She told us that the real name of Squaw Rock was: *The Rape of the Indian Tribes by the White Man.*

"My father planned the rock as part of a sanctuary he was building. He never told us what he had in mind, but it all seemed related to his feeling for the Indians. Further up the river, on a high cliff overlooking the valley, he built a pulpit (the cliff is still called Pulpit Rock), and on certain days he preached sermons from this cliff to the

101

congregated spirits of the thousands of Indians massacred by the settlers. It seems strange to us, but he was a spiritualist and these things had great meaning to him."

She arose. "Would you like to see my father's paintings?"

I looked at Arthur and he looked at me.

"P-paintings?" I said. "Did he paint, too?"

"Yes, he painted until the end of his days." Mrs. Sargent led us into the house and we saw the *Monkey Picture*, the *Self-Portrait* and a half dozen others. The *Monkey Picture* and a *View of Chagrin* hung in bedrooms and the *Self-Portrait* leaned against a basement wall.

When I was able to say anything, I said: "Did he do any other painting?"

"Yes, he painted a great many more. There are a few in the hands of relatives . . ."

"And the rest?" I asked. "Where are they?"

Mrs. Sargent looked at me very calmly. "I burned them," she said. "I burned nearly all of them."

"You burned them?"

"Yes," she said, "I had to. I had them in my house up on the hill and took good care of them for thirty years. Then I lost the house and moved down here. .You can see that there is no room for them here. Nobody liked them. Nobody wanted them. I didn't want them to fall into the hands of anybody who wouldn't take care of them. So I did what my father would have done. I destroyed them. All but these few. But I did take good care of them for thirty years."

And I had arrived three weeks too late.

From Henry Church's daughter and from many others, we learned a great deal about him.

His father, Henry, arrived in Chagrin Falls in 1834 to open the first blacksmith shop in this new settlement. They had travelled overland by wagon to Buffalo where they loaded their furniture onto the *Daniel Webster*. The *Daniel Webster* burned wood, tar and butter and finally began consuming itself. Henry, Sr., is supposed to have put out the fire and saved all lives.

On May 20, 1836, Henry Church, the painter, was born.

Henry was too frail and sickly to attend school, so his mother taught him and he was allowed to roam in the surrounding wilderness. He developed his solitary nature and learned to prefer the woods and streams. His daughter told me that he always regarded these years of separation from other children as decisive.

But his father ended this idyllic outdoor phase and put the thirteen-year-old boy to work as his apprentice. When young Henry took charcoals from his father's forge and drew on the white-washed walls of the shop, his father whacked him for it. In later years Henry always referred to his father as "a practical man and a good provider" and claimed that he inherited his artistic talent from his mother, who drew a little.

Henry married in 1861. The Civil War drove the town into a patriotic frenzy and out of its population of about 900, one hundred and eight men enlisted. But Henry, a spiritualist and a deeply religious man, bought his way out of the service for $400, which was permitted by the Government.

Many years later he painted a life-sized portrait of Abraham Lincoln, with the broken shackles of slavery at his feet, and an equestrian portrait of General Sherman.

102

He presented these portraits to the local G.A.R., but they immediately put the paintings into their cellar.

A photograph taken in 1870 shows Hank in the town band. He played the cornet, the alto horn and the banjo. He also played the harp and bass fiddle, both of which he made himself.

His father died in 1878 and Henry, finally freed of the parental censorship, took to painting, hunting, and sculpture in earnest. He retired at the age of fifty and rented out the blacksmith shop. The town never quite forgave him for this violation of its industrial code. It was quite apparent to everyone that this giant (he was six feet three and weighed over 200 pounds) was using far more strength and energy on his massive sculpture than was required in the shoeing of horses.

Church planted a tree on the town square and put a wrought-iron ring around it which read:

> On this tree let me be
> Until I do a century see.

He littered his front yard with his weird sculpture, all of it fitted with glass eyes supplied by a taxidermist. When the children molested his work, he is supposed to have fired shots in the air to scare them off.

It was in this period that Henry went to visit Archibald M. Willard, painter of the famous *Spirit of '76*. The Cleveland painter saw him a few times and sent him off with the address of a paint supply house in New York. This was Henry Church's only contact in his lifetime with another artist.

Church worked secretly on the Squaw Rock and quit when only partly through with his conception, because he was discovered. The word jumped to town and, on the following day, the entire population of Chagrin was out in force to see Hank's latest.

The tombstone, finished twenty years before his death, was kept out of the cemetery by the local trustees, who quite plainly stated that the lion was too ugly for their graveyard.

The fight went on for years and Henry Church finally won, when he announced that unless they allowed his memorial into the family plot, he would live forever! This threat overwhelmed the opposition and the lion was installed.

Having won this battle, Henry died in his seventy-second year on April 17, 1908. But his last victory was posthumous. Old Hank left a special list of people who were to attend his funeral. It is said that the sermon he delivered on the gramophone cylinder was a scathing denunciation of his enemies, especially the trustees of the cemetery.

When I arrived in Chagrin Falls in 1937, there were only a few fragments left of all his work. A vandal had knocked off part of his tombstone and it looked for a while as though the Chagrin River was going to undermine and destroy Squaw Rock. But his daughter wrote to the park authorities, and after much delay, a new base was built under the rock. The W.P.A. erected a beautiful new sign, telling about the blacksmith artist from Chagrin, and asking Boy Scouts and other young men not to deface the rock and to desist from the carving of initials on it.

On my second visit to Chagrin, I noticed that the tree in the town square had been chopped down. An obstruction to modern traffic, it never saw its century. Every day

103

for years his daughter performed a ritual act in connection with this tree. The children always pulled the wrought-iron ring off its nail and threw it into the mud. Each morning his daughter bent down, picked up the iron ring and replaced it upon its nail.

Mr. Rosenberg has in his Bronx apartment many of the paintings now extant by this individualist who was the despair of the community in which he lived. He amusingly relates the reactions to these paintings of his janitor, who, upon visiting the apartment, remarked: "Humph, primitives." The janitor was formerly watchman in a museum.

Self-Portrait

By rrs shape the canvas brings to mind the dying days of the 19th century when oval portraits hung in the front parlor. Conventional in shape, this is no conventional self-portrait, for Church has made some unusual inclusions.

The background of buff-gray-lavender is mistlike, and near the head of the artist the mist rises enough for a group of floating figures to become visible. They are his personal muses, and he has introduced them like a halo about his head. An arrangement of fruits and flowers ties up with them, all being held together by sharply creased, rather than curling, rose-colored ribbon which winds in and about, creating out of them a garland thrown over his shoulders.

The muses are depicted as masculine and feminine, and we notice Painting is connected with the eye, Music with the ear, (the harp and cello are faithful recordings of actual instruments which Church, himself, made) and the masculine muses of Sculpture and Smithing with the skull and temple respectively. The muse of Painting has just added the highlight to the eye, the final touch completing the portrait.

Wings form a part of the headdress of each, and they wear filmy drapes which flow in Victorian curlicues.

In the case of Smithing, we see that Church has given the same importance to this, his trade, as to his fine-art activities. No doubt he felt a strong

104

CHURCH *Self-Portrait.* c. 1900.   Collection Sam Rosenberg.

tie between them and fully realized how his trade had prepared him for sculpture. While he has indicated the mundane nature of the smith's calling—the foot of this muse is seen—he has at the same time exalted it by virtue of the crown placed upon its head. This crown displaces the traditional helmet of Vulcan which Church in turn has given to Sculpture.

The self-portrait is that of a strong and determined person with pride in his strength. The cap and beard give him the look of a patriarch. For all this imposing aspect of his appearance, his eyes sparkle and there are suggested smile wrinkles around them, which mark a genial side to his forceful personality. He is dressed in a modish brown lounging jacket with moire silk lapels and velvet collar and wears a deep blue shirt. His dark bow tie is edged with red piping and this red is faintly seen as it filters through the almost impenetrable beard.

In harmony with the picture frame, a series of arcs, one upon the other, rise to the top of the painting. Beginning with the line of the mouth, and then the mustache, they follow through the eyebrows, the hair-line, the crescent-like cap upon his head, the arched muses, and mist-like background, and finally the top line of the canvas. Some of these make complete ovals which work in from the picture frame: the configuration of the muses and still life, the oval of the face and the ear.

The Monkey Picture

IT DOES not require great imagination to believe that one of the reasons Church painted *The Monkey Picture* was to ridicule the abundance of staid Victorian fruit still-lifes that found their way even to remote sections of the country at the time colored lithography was first in flower.

With great disrespect and no little glee, he has literally turned the tables. The prize fruits assembled here in all their glorious colors, their bloom and lusciousness, are deliberately scattered, trampled upon and tumbled in all directions. Withal, they are tenderly treated as they remain uncrushed in the melee.

Its background decor is in the style of the early movies, and the Keystone cop fits perfectly into this analogy. We have entered the movie at a crucial moment, the high point of the action coming as a culmination of the preceding scenes. We missed the part where the monkeys escaped from their cage on the lawn, climbed through the window and discovered the table filled with "calendar" fruits. They grabbed for the only banana and the altercation began. The nimbler one got it, but before he was able to devour more than a bite, the fight grew hectic. At the very climax, we enter, and in this split second, the action freezes. It is this moment that the artist has caught, for in the next instant the wreckage would have been complete and the cop out of camera range.

Splashed by a cool dash of lemonade at the height of the excitement, the tiger rug is brought to life, only to suffer a more ignominious fate. For a monkey has anchored himself by firmly coiling his tail about the tiger's throat, and adding insult to injury, the jungle beast is about to be drowned if not crowned by the huge tumbling pitcher of lemonade heading his way. Two bright red strawberries have rolled down the tablecloth, and are flanking his either jowl with a temptation which he has no choice but to resist.

Other humorous twists are the double images, the largest being the profile of the watermelon which is also a face. This fruit is lusciously accented by tear-drop seeds which convey the sensation of dripping juice and whet the palate. Then there are markings on the surface of the canteloupe where the graining resembles ancient script which in part becomes familiar enough to spell out "H. Church, Pixt.—Painter."

The canvas is also signed at the bottom, not as a cryptogram, but plainly so that one may be more directly informed: "H. Church—Painter—Blacksmith."

Patterns on the wall and floor, markings on the monkeys, the tiger and the glassware, as well as on the fruits, form a galaxy of vibrations that heighten the excitement of the picture. The disarray, the tumbling bowls of fruit and sliding tablecloth simulate disorganization, yet the canvas is completely organized pictorially. The complexities of the arrangement and the subtle byplays are so numerous that only a few can be mentioned. Compositional obliques from opposite directions play against each other. One set leads into the picture via the slant of the curb outside the window. The movement of the approaching cop whose glittering regalia is painted in gilt, follows this

107

oblique, and his raised club arrests the eye. This gesture is mocked by the banana in the monkey's hand, and the oblique line of movement, following rapidly and abruptly along his arm, body, and tail, continues through the other monkey down the glass, his tail, and the tablecloth past the frightened tiger and out of the picture.

The counter-obliques are formed by the falling glassware on the table, and the movement of the spilling fruit.

Further, there are dynamic centers from which various movements radiate, such as the limbs and tails of both monkeys, the folds caused by the foot of the monkey clawing the tablecloth, the spray of lemonade out of the glass, as well as many others, less active.

Aside from the curb of the walk, there are many points of entrance into the action of the picture, for example up along the knife, or down either side of the wall panels, all of them leading into the action in such a way as to give a fresh plastic continuity. Along the latter route, one is led around the contour of the watermelon rind, and this rocking movement recurs in larger and smaller arcs upon the table.

Shadows and reflections are capriciously introduced. They are carried out in full detail, playing an important role in tying together the picture's forms. Pictorially they function with logic, but not in accordance with the science of light. The shadow of the knife passes over several planes such as the melon, tray, table-edge, table-side, and the floor itself. Still its contour faithfully parallels that of the knife with nary a break regardless of what plane it falls upon. This brings us to another irregularity. The table according to the knife is but half a knife high and the fruit which casts its shadows upon the floor pattern reaches almost to the table-top. In comparing the large peach and the tiger's head, both of them on the floor and on the same horizontal plane in the foreground, we find an appalling incongruity in scale. More than likely Church reduced his tiger skin to fit into the allotted floor space, and by the same token lifted his floor under the table to provide a rest within the picture frame for the still-life which has fallen from the table. These are liberties which, properly integrated, are often taken by creative artists. They reveal the resourcefulness of the inventive individual, whose picture logic is effectively coordinated with the means at his disposal, and are responsible for the strength and fascination of his work.

108

CH *The Monkey Picture.* c.1908.   Collection Sam Rosenberg.

Decoration on the facade of his grocery store on Mechanic St.,
New Hope

CHAPTER SEVEN

JOSEPH PICKETT

Jòseph Pickett was of a roving temperament, and for a great many years
followed the carnivals. But his travels took him no great distance and he returned to New Hope, Pa., each winter, which he spent telling stories about
his adventures. At these carnivals and fairs he had concessions, sometimes
cane racks, knife boards, but most frequently shooting galleries. He had a

110

flair for this kind of life, was an expansive, gregarious individual and loved to talk. He was well-liked and he prospered, especially with a rifle range he ran at Neshaminy Falls, a picnic grounds near New Hope, to which wealthy Philadelphians drove their carriages for Sunday outings.

A handsome man, "any photo of a Kentucky colonel would do to describe him," said a neighbor. In later years his wide mustache and wonderful shock of hair were completely white, except when he suddenly appeared with them dyed black; then they would gradually whiten again. Although he had never been to the South, his family originally came from there, and he had the grand manner of the Southern gentleman.

Edward Pickett, his father, had come to New Hope in 1840, eight years before Joseph was born, to repair the locks on one of the canals. He remained to build canal boats and his sons worked with him. Joseph, the youngest of four sons and one of a family of eight, learned this trade from his father, but he was only to spend a limited time at it.

Although he had this early training and did a great deal of manual work all his life, there is good evidence that he was not a master-craftsman; still, he was an ingenious man with ideas and the ability to carry them out. Among his many projects were two houses, one that he built on Dark Hollow Hill when he married in the mid-nineties; another, the addition to his second grocery store on Bridge Street. He made a pair of calfskin boots which were too tight but which he wore anyway. There exists a chest of drawers elaborately patterned in light wood marquetry, and a home-made barber chair, which nobody remembers being shaved in, was found in the back of his store after his death. This chair is crude but inventively made, with the back and arms hinged to the forelegs so that the back can be pushed forward to give the person sitting in it a lift when getting up.

At Neshaminy Falls, Pickett met a "pink and pretty girl" whom he married when he was about forty-five years of age, and settled down never to roam again, much to the surprise of his neighbors. Emily Pickett became the plump kindly woman with the gray pompadour who always said, "Anything Joe wants to do is all right." She sold all of Pickett's effects, with the exception of his paintings, after his death. They had no children.

In the first years of their marriage, Pickett opened a modest grocery and

111

general store on Mechanic Street, where he remained more than a dozen years. On the side of the building the Bull Durham Company had painted their famous bull. On the facade, Pickett placed a sign with his name on it— just "Pickett"—and below it near a window he painted a landscape containing a huge maple tree. This outdoor painting, a photograph of which appears at the chapter head, is now, faded and chipped, underneath layers of stucco. This was not Pickett's first attempt at painting, for Mrs. Turner, a retired equestrienne formerly with Barnum & Bailey's, remembers he had decorated his shooting galleries with landscapes and his knife boards and cane racks in "good old circus blue with gay curlicues."

For some years Pickett used house paint for his pictures, but later used regular artists' supplies, tubes of paint, brushes and a palette. Most of his pictures were painted in the back room of the store on Mechanic Street, where he used to invite one or two friends to see his work. These friends feel that he painted as a compensation for the quiet life he now led. He worked on each painting for years, adding the color continuously until he got his raised textures. In this connection, another neighbor, Mrs. Janney, recalls especially an incident about the flag in *Manchester Valley*. From time to time, he would ask her if she thought it was heavily enough painted, and she would say "Yes," but he would go right on adding more pigment until he was satisfied with the result. About this picture she also relates that one of her friends asked Pickett why he had painted a fence around the school when there hadn't been one there for years. He insisted it was still there, but he soon learned it was there only in his memory; for the fence had long been gone.

Pickett was an enterprising person, and in his general store sold everything including live bait and ammunition shells which he himself filled. He also rented out his gun for hunting.

In June, 1912, he bought a store next to the railroad station on Bridge Street, where he moved, building the addition for living quarters already mentioned. These buildings, the store and the house from the canal side, are the subject of his last known painting, *Sunset, Lehigh Canal, New Hope*. Mrs. Janney also recalls his working on this picture. The cement bridge in the painting was constructed in 1915, dating the canvas after this time. In

112

1919, several months after his death, the store was sold during the two-day sale of his effects, and is now Harry Worthington's Garage.

Lloyd Ney, New Hope artist, now owns the building on Mechanic Street where Pickett had his first grocery store, and it was Ney who bought the first Pickett paintings. In 1926 two were hung in Al Worthington's Garage and Ney purchased both for $15. The following year he traded them to Moore Price of New Hope for $50 worth of frames. It was here that Holger Cahill saw them, and Mr. Cahill introduced the work of Pickett to the public in a series of museum exhibitions. In the catalogue on American Folk Art, published by the Museum of Modern Art in 1932, Mr. Cahill tells of an early but unsuccessful attempt on the part of Pickett to have his work exhibited:

In the year of his death he was persuaded by a resident of the artist colony at New Hope to send one of his paintings to the Pennsylvania Academy exhibition, where it is said to have received three jury votes, those of William L. Lathrop, Robert Henri and Robert Spencer. After Pickett's death his paintings were put up at auction, but as they brought only a dollar apiece his widow bought them in, and gave the *Manchester Valley* to the New Hope High School where it hung for ten or twelve years.

The information in this biography has been gleaned from many of the older inhabitants of New Hope, who knew Pickett well, and it is interesting to note from the material gathered that men remember Joseph Pickett as one who could do anything with tools, a "handy man," while women recall his picturesque side, his adventurous spirit and non-conformist ways and habits of dress; and they remember facts about his painting.

Manchester Valley

THE TOPOGRAPHY of the country painted by Joseph Pickett makes it inevitable that everything in the picture follow a cascading movement. The hills against the sky beginning at the upper right sweep across and down into the ravine at the left. This cascading movement is frontal as well as lateral as the contours of the land approach the bottom of the canvas. The stream follows the natural bent of the country in a series of waterfalls and rapids and both shorelines emphasize the descent. In a flowing movement tracks and train also parallel this direction, and buildings and homes throughout the composition adjust themselves to the general movement of the land descending in *Manchester Valley*.

Formal perspective gives way to a personal perspective and objects of greater importance to the artist are given greater scale regardless of distance. The school, which is in the background, is largest, while the factories in the foreground, although they are taller buildings, are reduced. The importance of the schoolhouse is obvious. Apart from its size, there is its commanding position near the crest of the hill, where it is topped by a huge belfry and a flag flying at the highest point in the picture. And further, the schoolhouse is enclosed by a heart-shaped fence and is surrounded by a sulphurous green area that creates around it the effect of glowing light.

But apart from this there are compositional reasons for the difference in scale between the buildings. For instance, the factories in the foreground if larger would have cut off a great deal of the view.

The wind creates a resistance or countermovement to the topography of the country for it blows the flag, the clouds, the branches of the trees silhouetted against the sky and the smoke from the train, in the opposite direction. By the stream below, trees are again silhouetted, this time against the flowing water, where they seem to be held in place as much by the current as by the shelter of the valley.

One of the most striking elements in the picture is the use of textures to give wherever this is possible the tactile experience of the material represented. Sand, shell and other gritty substances have been mixed with the

114

ETT *Manchester Valley.*   Collection The Museum of Modern Art.

pigment to gain the desired results. For example, the foundation in the trestle has the feel of cement to the touch,* and in the center house near the tracks, concrete, native rock and brick are all simulated. The bark of the trees is built up to high relief primarily to give volume, but none the less to give the proper texture.

On the train are two tiny figures, the only ones in the picture: a fireman and a conductor. They are modeled in half-round relief and are reminiscent of toy figures on a miniature railway. As a matter of fact the entire picture is like a toy village of the Revolutionary period with the fanciful anachronistic interjection of a railroad and a 48-star flag.

Reflections are introduced under the trestle where tree trunks and concrete piers are seen in the quiet water. The reflection of the bridge itself however is omitted as are all shadows throughout the picture. This omission is particularly striking in the case of the train which casts no shadow upon the tracks.

Fences play in and out of the trees and around the houses, acting as ties which bind together pictorially the various space divisions in the composition. The railroad tracks, too, become a part of this fence pattern but here knocked down so that they may properly function as tracks.

Although the engine is in profile, the full circle of its front elevation is seen, adding to the sensation of travel or motion by including the experience of an oncoming view. This conception doubles the hazard of a shaky train upon an unsteady roadbed, leaving the spectator hoping against hope but expecting the worst as the train nears the curve over the trestle.

Pickett's fresh and vibrant color, inventive handling of forms and surfaces, diverse compositional arrangement, are so completely coordinated with the originality of his concept, that *Manchester Valley* becomes an outstanding painting achievement.

* Utrillo as early as 1912 mixed plaster and cement in his pigment, in an effort more closely to approximate the surfaces of foundations and walls of buildings in his Paris scenes.

GREGORIO VALDES, Key West

CHAPTER EIGHT

GREGORIO VALDES

THREE PICTURES, not only signed but addressed as well, hung on the wall of the inner sanctum of Hugh Stix behind his Artists' Gallery in Eighth Street. By mere accident I saw them but it was no accident that I liked them. For if they narrowly escaped the clichés of Cuban picture postcards, it was

117

miraculous to see how they had avoided falling into the limbo of cheap sentimentality. Although very Cuban-travelogue in color and feeling, they were direct and honest in statement, substantially painted, and possessed of a rarefied spirit that isolated them from the taint of cheapness.

Mr. Stix informed me that G. Valdes was a Cuban-American sign-painter and also a "mail-order artist," who painted pictures from postcards sent him by customers. This was no doubt the reason he put his address on his work. His paintings were in effect also business cards.

The pictures haunted me, so I decided to look for what was likely to be a suitable subject for him to paint. To ask an artist to make a picture to order was a new experience for me. In the Latin-American section of Harlem, the neighborhood of 116th Street and Fifth Avenue, I sought a picture of buildings with architectural details of the type he might best understand, but being unable to find one, selected instead a colored photograph of a very Spanish bouquet of roses.

This I sent to Valdes with a money order and a request that he make a painting of it. It was early in 1939. Many weeks later, although it seemed interminably longer, a postcard came from Valdes asking me to excuse the delay, for he had not been well, but would soon finish the painting. I was never to receive the bouquet of roses.

Later, in April, the Artists' Gallery had a small but very interesting show of his work in their rear gallery. There were fifteen oils, several of them splendid little canvases. A street scene called *Monument to José Marti* was brilliantly painted, almost a *grisaille*, with a single surprise color note, mustard. In the middle of the street, next to the pedestal on which the statue of José Marti stood, a stepladder was placed, which suggested that perhaps José kept working hours and used the ladder to step down after his daily stint. Some of the paintings, in fact most of them, were made from pictures which obviously awoke no response in the artist, for they were widely separated in merit from the ones that did ring true.

On May 17th, the following letter came from Valdes' daughter, Mrs. Juanita Valdes Montejo:

... My father passed away the 9th of this month. He was preparing your work when he became ill and got worse in about four days. I am sending you some photographs of works he left. In case you like any of them I will send them or if you prefer the money you had sent him. Please answer as soon as possible so I may know what to do about your money.

Not long after, the paintings arrived and soon they were all spoken for by friends and by myself. At this time Mrs. Montejo wrote:

. . . I am very sorry I do not have more paintings. I thank you heartily for your interest in my father's paintings. . . . I regret that my father could not participate personally in all this triumph, as he would have been very happy. Well that's destiny. . . .

Valdes lived obscurely for sixty years, and just as he reached the threshold of recognition, he passed away.

Elizabeth Bishop, who lives in Key West, wrote a most sympathetic article about him in the summer issue of *Partisan Review*, 1939. Excerpts including biographical material which Miss Bishop obtained from Valdes himself, are quoted here:

GREGORIO VALDES, 1879-1939

By ELIZABETH BISHOP

The first painting I saw by Gregorio Valdes was in the window of a barber-shop on Duval Street, the main street of Key West. The shop is in a block of cheap liquor stores, shoe-shine parlors and poolrooms, all under a long wooden awning shading the sidewalk. The picture leaned against a cardboard advertisement for Eagle Whiskey, among other window decorations of red and green crepe-paper rosettes and streamers left over from Christmas and the announcement of an operetta at the Cuban school,— all covered with dust and fly-spots and littered with termites' wings.

It was a view, a real View, of a straight road diminishing to a point through green fields, and a row of straight Royal Palms on either side, so carefully painted that one could count seven trees in each row. In the middle of the road was the tiny figure of a man on a donkey, and far away on the right the white speck of a thatched Cuban cabin that seemed to have the same mysterious properties of perspective as the little dog in Rousseau's *The Cariole of M. Juniet*. The sky was blue at the top, then white, then beautiful blush pink, the pink of a hot, mosquito-filled tropical evening. As I went back and forth in front of the barber-shop on my way to the restaurant, this picture charmed me, and at last I went in and bought it for three dollars.*

. . . He lived at 1221 Duval Street, as it said on all his pictures, but he had a "studio" around the corner in a decayed, unrentable little house. There was a palette nailed to one of the posts of the verandah with *G. Valdes, Sign Painter* on it.

. . . Gregorio was very small, thin and sickly, with a childish face and tired brown eyes,—in fact he looked a little like the *Self Portrait* of El Greco. He spoke very little

* Reproduced, Page 125.

English but was so polite that if I took someone with me who spoke Spanish he would almost ignore the Spanish and always answer in English, anyway, which made explanations and even compliments very difficult. He had been born in Key West, but his wife was from Cuba, and Spanish was the household language, as it is in most Key West Cuban families. . . . He had five daughters, two sons, and three grandchildren.

I commissioned him to paint a large picture of the house I was living in. . . . When he delivered this picture there was no one at home, so he left it on the verandah leaning against the wall. As I came home that evening I saw it there from a long way off down the street,—a fair sized copy of the house, in green and white, leaning against its green and white prototype. In the gray twilight they seemed to blur together and I had the feeling that if I came closer I would be able to see another miniature copy of the house leaning on the porch of the painted house, and so on,—like the Old Dutch Cleanser advertisements.

. . . In this picture (a still life) the paint had cracked slightly, and examining it I discovered one eccentricity of Gregorio's painting. The blue background extended all the way to the table top and where the paint had cracked the blue showed through the fruit. Apparently he had felt that since the wall was back of the fruit he should paint it there, before he could go on and paint the fruit in front of it.

. . . This story is told by Mr. Edwin Denby in his article on Valdes for the Artists' Gallery exhibition: "When he was a young man he lived with an uncle. One day when that uncle was at work, Valdes took down the towel rack that hung next to the washbasin and put up instead a painting of the rack with the towel on it. When the uncle came back at five, he went to the basin, bent over and washed his face hard and still bent over he reached up for the towel. But he couldn't get hold. With the water streaming into his eyes, he squinted up at it, saw it and clawed at it, but the towel wouldn't come off the wall. 'Me laugh plenty, plenty,' Valdes said. . . ."

Edwin Denby and Rudolph Burckhardt, both of New York, found Valdes on a trip to Key West, and Mrs. Montejo mentions in letters that they had been his friends for some time. They own most of his paintings.

Here we have the recorded experiences of four individuals with an obscure self-taught artist. There were others who also participated, and in each case it is likely that the pleasure which such experiences give and the delight in sharing them with others, were theirs. To taste the excitement of discovering self-taught artists is not necessarily for the isolated person, but is an experience that can belong to anyone who will but look around.

120

Paris Scene

HERE WE have the actual photograph from which Valdes worked, and the painting which he made from it. It is a scene of Paris, and Valdes, never having been in France, changed it into terms consistent with his own environment and understanding. As a result the painting, through the eyes of this Cuban-American, is Spanish in flavor rather than French. Tiled rooftops replace shingles, and the cold grey aspect of the Paris photo, interesting as it is, reappears as a clean urban setting, sharply accented by a strong sun. Valdes retains his inner vision of Florida skies.

It would seem that the hundreds of smokestacks in the photo have challenged the credulity of the resident of Key West, where because of climate, he has had little contact with such a phenomenon. He has eliminated them as if they were exaggerations, and used only the few that must have seemed logical to him.

The artist's selection is in fact evident at every turn, and his transpositions from photograph to canvas produce in every case great simplification. The bottom of the photo cuts off the store fronts and awning tops, and the contact of buildings with earth is established indirectly, by suggestion, whereas in the painting the buildings are planted squarely upon the earth. The artist has created a foundation not only for the buildings, but for the composition as well. While the photographic shot is subtle, the painting is disarmingly direct.

There was, altogether, no inclination to copy what he saw, for what he saw he was unable to comprehend: it involved complex perspectives and receding planes quite foreign to Valdes. He has reduced the photo's maze of facet-planes, to three horizontal planes in general: foreground, middle and background. For instance, the three buildings directly behind the Hotel Edgar Quinet are straightened from their sharply angular Z formation so as to appear on the same plane. Two of these buildings which heretofore stood at right angles to each other, are now covered by the straight line of a common roof, unbroken except for the vertical of a smokestack. The four garret windows in the building forming the middle line of the Z have been omitted, probably because they presented to the artist the problem of converting their oblique lines to fit in with the new horizontalism of the roof.

121

Paris Scene: Photograph from which the painting was made.

122

DES *Paris Scene.*   Collection Orson Welles.

123

Valdes may have begun his picture at the right and proceeded to the left, for we find that the space is less accurately oriented to the photograph as the picture nears the frame on the left. His procedure here is very much like inexpert sign-painting. If a sign-painter fails to make a lay-out in advance, he may either have to crowd or omit the remainder of his message as he nears the end of his space. However, in the picture, this seeming irregularity imparts a feeling of natural growth.

All of the printed signs have been ignored and omitted except the name of the hotel. French signs make little sense to Valdes, the Cuban-American sign-painter.

Cuban Landscape

Miss Bishop has already given a general description of this painting.

The picture is exceedingly small, but the scale does not diminish the grandeur of the palms nor confine the nostalgic expanse of space. The configuration of the man and the donkey is that of a tiny pendant set jewel-like in the landscape.

Light reflected from the evening sky silhouettes the dark-green palms. Strangely, from the opposite direction, where the observer stands, another light enters the picture, as if the artist stood at the head of the road, his eyes shining upon it like automobile headlights. In looking along the road we see that all the trees on either side are lit up on the inside by these "headlights." Brilliant at the picture frame, this light diffuses as it travels up the road.

Curiously enough, neither trees nor figures cast shadows. One may well believe that the light emanating from the sky equals that which shines in from the foreground, and shadows become neutralized. Photographers often play one light against the other when they wish to eliminate shadows. It is hardly possible, though, that Valdes used such a sophisticated device. Shadows do not appear simply because it probably never occurred to him to use them. His use of light gives to the picture the mysterious effect of an inner light in a natural world—the isolation of the artist's vision.

124

ALDES *Cuban Landscape.* Collection Elizabeth Bishop, Key West.

Southernmost House in U.S., Key West, Florida

THE HORIZONTAL quality of *Southernmost House*, one of its most prominent pictorial characteristics, can be attributed to Valdes' occupation as a provincial artisan, and his geographical environment—topographically flat Key West.

The setting is a corner plot where, as a matter of fact, two streets meet at right angles. Three trees along the curb are on the side street, the house is on the front street and the pillar near the trees marks the corner. Valdes has straightened these streets to within a degree of making a continuous thoroughfare of them. The line of the stone wall is altogether straight, stretching across the entire canvas, and the hedge atop it becomes the horizon line of the painting.

By the same token the house itself has been completely flattened out so that it too remains on the same plane. In life, the house is deeper than it is wide, but in the painting Valdes has made it all into one virtually solid front. Therefore we can distinguish front from side not by perspective but only by detail.

The upper verandah over the main door we know to be frontal; the tall windows we accept as the side. Still the floorline of the upper verandah and the underscoring beneath the side windows are a continuous line, placing the facade and side of the house on one frontal plane.

The picture is filled with the brilliant sunlight of the southland. Bleached blue skies and sharp accents on the house and vegetation enhance the bright effect.

As we have already observed, Valdes either ignores or discards shadows. In *Southernmost House*, we are aware of the position of the sun by the highlighting on the tree trunks and it is apparent that if shadows were used, they would have had to fall obliquely across the sidewalk and wall. And then the inclusion of slanting shadows would have disturbed the horizontal composition.

Each window is given its own entity and each differs from the next in

126

SOUTHERNMOST. HOUSE. IN. U.S. KEY. WEST. FLORIDA.

G VALDES
1221 DUVAL ST

size, shape and color. The front windows are wider and reflect the blue of the skies. This somehow increases the flatness of the architecture since one is given the illusion of seeing through the house to the sky beyond. On the side, also, the windows make the house appear empty, but this time it is the dark emptiness of a haunted house. However, the house is not deserted, and notice to this effect seems to be served by the formation of the tiger-marked palm trees whose trunks spell out the hospitable word IN. (*Southernmost House* takes in "paying guests").

To incorporate a lettered legend is traditional in Spanish painting of the old world as well as the new. This is done generally across the bottom of the picture, and Valdes, by adding his address, has converted it to a business use.

127

MOTHER MOSES in her "studio."

CHAPTER NINE

ANNA MARY ROBERTSON MOSES

THE ANCESTORS of "Mother" Moses were Scottish, Irish and English. They came to this country at different times between 1740 and 1830, all of them settling in the immediate vicinity of southern Washington County, New York State. In their time, several served in the War of the Revolution.

Coming from what her brother calls a prolific "foundation stock," she was one of a family of ten; her mother was one of eleven; her grandfather, of fifteen; while her husband was one of a family of twelve children.

128

The following is her own engaging account of her life:

I was born in 1860 near the village of Greenwich in the section known as the Cottrell neighborhood, my ancestors were early settlers in Cambridge, my Great Great Grandfather Archibald Elexander Robertson was a wagon maker, and made the first wagon to run over the old Cambridge turnpike.

He hewed it out with an axe and a saw, He came from Scotland in 1776 or there about, they were soldiers in the revolution, my Father moved to Easton when I was a small child.

I was married November 9, 1878, on that date I married Thomas Solomon Moses, a grandson of the famous Dr. Moses and together we left for North Carolina, However we never reached there, we got as far as Staunton Virginia, where we planned to stay over the week end, and there we were kidnapped, that is the people persuaded us to settle there in the middle of the Shenandoah Valley, and there we lived for more than twenty years, In 1905 we returned north, where my husband died Jan. 15, 1927. I live with my youngest son who cares for the farm. I have five children and eleven Grandchildren and one great Granddaughter, I also brought up a niece,

When I was quite small my Father would get me and my Brothers white paper by the sheet, It was used in those days for newspapers, He liked to see us draw pictures, it was a pennie a sheet, and it lasted longer than candy,

My oldest Brother loved to draw Steam engines, that was a great hobby with him, the next Brother went in for animals, But as for my self I had to have pictures and the gayer the better, I would draw the picture and then color it with grape juice or berries any thing that was red and pretty in my way of thinking Once I was given some carpenters red and blue chalk, Then I was *rich*, But children did not have so much in those days, and we appreciated what we did get,

Then came the days when I dabbled in oil paints and made my *lamb scapes* as my Brother said I called them, they had some brilliant sun sets, and Father would say Oh not so bad, But Mother was more practical, thought that I could spend my time other ways, Then in school the teacher would give us maps to draw, and I would make the mountains in my own way, the teacher liked them, and would ask if he might keep them,

Then long years went by, one day my daughter asked me to make her a worsted picture, she had seen one and liked it and thought I could do one better, I made and gave away many of these, Then I commenced to paint with oil,

Mother Moses

In print, one loses the charm of the unexpected capital letters, of the commas for periods as though she were breathlessly talking, for these are of a piece with the very formation of her Victorian script.

It is surprising to find that there should have been a lapse of almost seventy years during which Mother Moses did no painting at all. The business of growing up, of raising a family, and the countless chores of farm life are

129

perhaps the reasons for it. And so it was not until she was seventy-seven that she took up painting again. Using a piece of canvas that had been left over from mending a threshing-machine cover, she painted her first oil with old house paints which she found in the barn. Pleased with the result, she sent to Sears Roebuck for mail-order "artists' supplies," colors and brushes, and set about painting in earnest.

Let it not be thought that she has given up her routine work-a-day schedule, for she fits her painting time in between her daily tasks. Of these she writes:

One hardly stops canning up vegetables, then we have to can up meats for the summer use, and that is what I will be doing tomorrow, a right greasy job,

but so nice when it is all done, it makes one feel rich on the farm,

I wonder some times if there is any rest for the weary, no sooner than the butchering is out of the way then New Years, then a wedding to tend, don't you wish you were me,

Her jellies have won prizes at the County Fair, although her paintings submitted to the same fair received no recognition. Her other activities are no more nor less than baking and cooking for the household, gardening, house-cleaning and in-between-times, she finds that such tasks as wall-papering rooms or caring for one of the family babies are to be taken in one's stride.

On a visit to the Moses farm, we found her playing nurse to the infant of the niece whom she had raised. Still this did not interfere with her culinary duties—at tea-time we partook of fresh muffins, wild strawberry preserves, and for good measure cocoanut layer cake, all made by her own hands. Still there is time for her to work in oils and when the light is bad, she turns to her needlework—"worsted pictures."

Small and slim, Mother Moses is a tiny dynamo. Darting about with a surprisingly springy step, she is always ready for fun; her keen wit and animated response are trigger-fast.

The first public appearance of the work of Mother Moses was in the window of a country drug store. The second, which launched her official career as an artist, was in 1939, a few years later, when the exhibition of *Unknown American Painters* included three of her oils. At the time the show was current, I received the following letter from her:

I wish to thank you for the trouble that you have taken in my pictures, it was nice of you. Too bad that you had none better, I call those poor. I have some that I think good, that is in my way of thinking. But you have done fine, and I wish you the best of success, A friend as ever, Mother Moses

A year later she was to have her first "one-man" show, which was arranged by Louis Caldor and held at the St. Etienne Gallery in New York. She has had subsequent exhibitions at Gimbel Bros., and other department stores in the East.

Mother Moses paints as easily and naturally as a bird flies. Her work, very uneven, at times has great pictorial charm, at others, levels off to water-mill-and-thatched-cottage effects. She is unpredictable in her preferences. She may choose one kind or the other, but in any event, she is always full of humor and does not hesitate to twit herself about her choice. When a subject is particularly close to her, this immediately registers in her work. Possessed of a spontaneous and ingenuous compositional sense, a fresh spirit, and an aptitude for color luminosity, she gives to her best work a pictorial quality that is sprightly and distinctively American.

She paints on composition board, canvas, cardboard, and at one time was very fond of painting on the smooth surface of oilcloth. Never using an easel, she prefers to paint with her pictures resting on her knee against the edge of the table. She likes to have her pictures framed before she begins them. This she explains with a twinkle in her eye: "They are sort of undressed if they don't have frames on."

Home

MOTHER MOSES has instinctively made of this painting her own tree-of-life. The horizontal road spreading across the picture is like the great roots of a tree, and the short thick vertical road is the sturdy tree trunk from which the living quarters branch to the right and the barns to the left.

Enshrined within the fork of these branches is a small green island in the shape of a heart. Love of soil, love of landscape, love of home, all this is reflected in *Home* and Mother Moses has given us this love-motif in the heart-shaped green island.

She knows the trees, hills, flowers, and the green fields, all of which reflect the luminosity of the autumnal sunset. The bright red chimneys on the living quarters are nestled in the trees like ripe apples on the bough.

She understands distance by changing light. In the very foreground at the bottom of the canvas, the shadows are already heavy and the colors are in tonalities of mauve grey and darkened flower notes. In the middle area there is the even light of late afternoon, in which the greens brighten imperceptibly as they approach the hills. Here the sudden contrast of a layer of dark green hills is like an abyss dividing her land from the distant mountains, which are bathed in the atmospheric blues of lingering sunlight. The cloudless sky blends from warm delicate lavenders to cool faint sky blues.

The mauve brown barns and white houses are covered in common with roofs of grey, and nestled comfortably in the landscape. They are seen through trees which have discreetly shed their foliage in order to allow the eye to pass through them and observe important details in the buildings behind. The row of yellowing green trees on the lawn in front of the home does not conceal any of its windows. Every window, being important, is visible to the observer. The russet tree in front of the barn has shed its own skeleton of branches in order to allow a view of the structure. It is as if the observer had been endowed with heightened visual powers, with his eyes x-raying those obstacles placed by nature in the path of his vision.

Mother Moses, the oldest living member of her family, and her youngest grandchild stand at the foot of her tree-of-life. Since painting *Home*, a new member, her first great-grandchild, has arrived to increase the Moses clan by one generation.

SES *Home.* 1940

Sugaring Off

Sugaring Off is a picture of family reunion. Here are the children and the grandchildren of the Moses menage. Each participates in the maple sugar making. The *sugaring off* comes early in the Spring after timbering is finished and before the ground is ready for the plow. The sap must be boiled down the day it is gathered, since, like milk, it easily sours. This is why every available member of the family takes part. Each has his chores and the work progresses methodically. We feel the whole of it to be a job shared and well done, each individual knowing his part.

The two fires, on which pots of sap boil, and the tub on the ground over which the man bends, become a hub toward which all paths converge. Ox-drawn sleds in the distance approach along a path which leads out of the hills, and move toward the fire behind the trees. Diagonally opposite and entering from the lower right-hand corner of the picture, a team of horses brings a load of wood in the direction of the nearer fire. The boiling pot above it is supported by a log-arm along the line of which three figures converge toward this same fire. At the left the figures form an arc which swings in toward the skimmer who is pouring the sugar-wax into a tub of clean snow. Around the tub are gleeful children waiting for the sugar to cool so that they may have some.

Mother Moses stands in the doorway of the log cabin, but just for a moment, since the smoking chimney tells us she has culinary duties to perform inside.

The scale of the figures from foreground to remote distance, their placing against the snow, the intimacy with which the personality of each is depicted, and the genre character and spirit of the whole, make of this picture a New England "Breughel."

Representing a white horse on white snow is no problem to Mother Moses. By reverse process she silhouettes the white form of the animal upon a large evergreen which acts as a screen against which the horse becomes visible.

134

es *Sugaring Off.* 1940

Color notes in red, yellow, green, orange and blue are cheerful accents on the frosty snow. There is a sparkle in the snow as though it had just fallen. While the paint was still wet, Mother Moses sprinkled it with tiny particles of "star-dust" (a finely flaked mica which Victorian ladies dusted into their evening coiffures), and these catch the light and glisten as one moves before the canvas.

We look forward to the next family reunion. Up to now, three generations have carried on the work of *sugaring off*. Now that there are four generations, we will not be surprised to find a proportionate increase in the activity surrounding this traditional event.

The Cambridge Valley

AN INDIAN SUMMER landscape, *The Cambridge Valley*, includes the Moses land and all of the adjacent country to the north and west. Mother Moses, knowing every inch of it, spreads it like a patchwork quilt made up of swatches of light fields and dark woods, seamed with winding roads and streams and thin rows of hedges. The figures, animals, farmhouses are tiny toy-like ornaments set upon the quilt.

Beyond are the mountains which are described on the reverse side of the painting as follows:

to the far north west is mt. Equinox. to the far south East is the Berkshire Hills, next battlefield park mountain, next van ness Hill. next Oak Hill. in the centre—mt. Tom, and the owl Kill, to the west Oak hill range

The dark and light greens of the hill in the upper center just before the mountain range make a huge turtle's back in both pattern and shape.

Autumnal colors already spot the woods, and the harvest tans of piled cornstalks and the seared greens of stubbled fields tell of summer's end. The Moses farm, set in the left foreground on a web-like fabric of fields lies in the cradle of the valley.

The cloud patterns are particularly active for Moses, whose skies are usually pacific. This movement complements the undulations in the landscape.

136

ES *The Cambridge Valley.* 1939

137

ISREAL LITWAK coloring *Triboro Bridge.* Now in the Collection of M. Martin Janis, Buf

CHAPTER TEN

ISREAL LITWAK

ISREAL LITWAK lives in the East Flatbush section of Brooklyn and calls his modest bedroom his "little museum." It is filled with pictures from floor to ceiling, and they overflow frame to frame onto the furniture and floor. All of them are Litwaks—colored crayon and pencil on board "done in a secret technique." Litwak is a roomer and the enthusiasm for art is confined to his own room, for the rest of the apartment is pictureless.

138

Litwak is a jovial old man who likes to talk about art, especially his own art. Some time ago someone told him his work was "like Rousseau's." Never having heard the name, he was curious to learn about a man who painted like himself and he went to the library to investigate. Upon inquiry he was handed several books on the artist but a hasty examination of the reproductions made it clear to him that there was no resemblance at all. The reproductions were of the work of the Barbizon artist Theodore Rousseau. Later however, he did see Douanier Rousseau's work, and at that time exclaimed, "This is more like it. This is good work, very good work, plenty to criticize, but all right."

Litwak has sent the following letter covering the "highlights" of his life:

Born in Odessa, Russia in 1868. Became apprentice to a cabinet maker at age 11. Served in the Russian Army 4 yrs (21 to 25). Never had any lessons in drawing or painting. Came to the U.S.A. in 1903 with my family consisting of my wife and 2 children.

My other work in addition to cabinet making was varnishing furniture. Being occupied in work of this type one has to produce, that means hard work. Hard work means fatigue and need of rest.

Never did I give a thought to draw or design. Providing for the family, raising the children, those were uppermost in my mind. However on my day of rest and during holidays my greatest delight was to visit museums and marvel at the fine work of the old masters. As a matter of fact any artistic creation, sculpture, bronze figures, have always attracted my attention. I am a lover of good classical music and opera has a great effect on me.

At the age of 68 was unable to hold on to the sort of work I did, forced to retire. Not being used to idleness and to occupy my time with anything I suddenly had an urge to do some drawing and followed it up with painting. I tried oil paint, water color, and crayon. I was pleased with the result of the crayon work. I did some landscape. Some time later I produced two landscape pictures and thought of bringing them to the Brooklyn Museum for approval.

At that time Mr. Schneiwind was the curator of the dept. of drawings and prints. He was delighted with the work submitted to the directors for approval. The directors recognized me as an artist. In November 1939 I had 36 pictures completed and I was honored by the directors of the Brooklyn Museum by giving my work a special one-man exhibit. Of course you know how the critics acclaimed the exhibit, I will not elaborate on this phase. If a painting is good it must be admired and usually is. One achieves good painting by imagination, talent, patience and a lot of hard hard work, detail composition, proper colors.

Many components in the work of Litwak have the direct and elemental character of child art, particularly the symbol for the sun and the general

139

compositional sense. Together with this we find inventiveness in the creation of specific pictorial devices, and in the design of objects. Outstanding are his feeling for architecture, and his drawing of figures in amiable caricature. His freshness of expression gives his pictures spontaneity in spite of the very deliberate procedure he goes through to make them.

He works very long and hard on each picture, first making a full-sized drawing on paper and then carefully tracing it on cardboard. The design made by the deeply impressed lines is then filled in with colored crayon, giving the picture the general effect of tooled leather. After applying fixative and shellac, he waxes the pictures almost as if they were pieces of furniture, and frames them behind glass.

Litwak says of the figures in his paintings: "They are motion figures!" In speaking of his landscapes: "I look at it just to get an idea; then I go home and make it the way I want it, not the way it is." And again: "It was not like that—it was some kind of park but I made a better one."

The one-man show at the Brooklyn Museum brought many press notices and an Associated Press story that was widely published. Litwak treasures these clippings as he does the complete photographic record of his work which the Brooklyn Museum presented to him at that time.

Fifth Avenue

LITWAK INSISTED on directing attention to the bright yellow color that wings directly over the trees and the buildings in his *Fifth Avenue*. "This is the light of the world and above it comes the sky," he said, and pointing to the horizon line indicating the end of the retreating avenue: "The earth can never touch the sky but goes into the light of the world." All of Litwak's scenes have this light depicting the earth's atmosphere in some way, but here it is so pronounced that it becomes tangible and resembles distant mountains. This unique way of seeing is reflected in everything he makes.

The steep lines of traffic which first attract the eye are most amusingly conceived. Motor cars traveling uptown are unorganized, but the downtown traffic approaches in train-like fashion. Completely regimented in line, they are telescoped as though the driver of the front car unexpectedly jammed on his brakes. Added to the general hubbub, as an increased hazard to driving, the cars along the curb are precariously tilted in the scooped out saucer-like street.

The strolling figures on either sidewalk are decked out in their Sunday best. Their faces resemble those of ancient Sumerians, all in profile save one. As one seeks out this exception, the picture becomes a sort of esthetic game, full of the unexpected, and invites the observer to participate in the playing of it. Only a few of the clues will be given here.

The row of buildings to the right is compacted into a many-faceted cabinet. The variously sized blue windows set in the yellow, burnt sienna, grey, tan and white facades, are flutings, and the cornices and other trims make decorations of carving and marquetry to adorn this cabinet-maker's architecture. This effect is due in no small measure to the embossed surfaces which come from Litwak's technique of tracing from a drawing with deeply incised lines. As a point in the game the observer is asked to identify the facade-in-search-of-a-building.

This row of buildings, ever exceptional, recedes into deep space but not by formal diminishing perspective, as the height of the individual stories on the distant buildings is more or less the same as those in the foreground.

141

Litwak invents his own recession by reducing the number of stories of his buildings; the retreating steps of the roofs in relation to the line of the curb create the illusion of distance. All that remains of the final building is but a single story. The structures increasingly encroach upon the sidewalk and by the time we reach the last house, egress is cut off completely.

It is obvious that Litwak drew in the figures after the architecture had been built. The people are oriented to the sidewalk space. For a two-fold reason, he does not allow them to overlap the buildings: his beloved architecture must retain its inviolability, and yet it would never do for the people to be marred by the deeply incised architectural lines.

The two oncoming women are poised on the curb since they must find room for themselves within the angles formed by the buildings and the curb. Further forward the figures are not troubled with this problem—they have more headroom.

On the other side of the street the red brick wall divides the walk from the park and controls the pedestrians the same way the architecture does. The people in the foreground move about freely but as the walk narrows those further along are crowded to the other edge. Finally where little room is left, the last three unhappy figures are sandwiched between snugly parked cars at the curb.

The stylized design of the trees in the park and their color remind one of the inexpensive Numdah Indian rugs sold at department stores. The lampposts set amidst the trees diminish in height as they recede, but all of their lights remain the same size.

Another part of the game may be noted in the drawing of the branches of the two trees at the extreme left. The trees are in the park considerably beyond the wall, and still their branches extend in front of the lamppost at the curb. The very amusing engraving by Hogarth which tests one's powers of observation is brought to mind. It is filled with perspective oddities and is titled *Burlesque Perspective*. With Hogarth this game is one of conscious burlesque presented for the amusement of the knowing observer and is intended to destroy the pictorial values in his engraving. With Litwak's painting, seriously conceived, it is humor unconsciously born of a personal way of seeing, and ably integrated, that creates authentic pictorial means.

142

WAK   *Fifth Avenue.* 1940

CHAPTER ELEVEN

PATSY SANTO

As POINTED out in the opening chapter of the book, I have found that most self-taught artists reach full maturity with the painting of their first picture. This is so in spite of the fact that the level of their achievement thereafter is sometimes very uneven. Patsy Santo, however, is an interesting exception, since his work shows a development somewhat similar to that of artists who have studied. Influenced by calendars and chromos, his first paintings were of sentimental subjects and his technique and color were in keeping with

144

them. His technique today is more controlled and knowing, his color less sweet and more perceptive, his rendering of nature less picturesque and more pictorial. He still occasionally lapses into moments of esthetic weakness, but the trend is generally upward toward a growing fullness of meaning.

Despite the verisimilitude in his work, he does not copy nature, but invests it with a blending of poetic Italian sentiment and New England austerity.

The artist writes this brief account of his life:

Patsy Santo, born in Corsano, Italy, Dec. 25, 1893; son of Prof. Nicola and Cristina (Scrascia) Santo, a school professor. Came to America in 1913, making Albany, N. Y. first location; working for a short time as laborer for the D & H R R Co. Going from there to Hoosick Falls, N. Y. to work in Wood's Foundry. Later to North Adams, Mass. to work in the Print Works. Then going to Greenwich, N. Y. to work in a brush factory. In 1917 made Bennington, Vt. permanent residence where the next nine years were divided in working for the Bennington Brush factory, the EZ Waist Co. as cutter, and the Holden Leonard Co. as a weaver. Between jobs as housepainter. Never studied painting under anyone or at any school.

From information compiled during several visits with Patsy Santo, (whose name was given to me by the artists, Elsa and Stefan Hirsch) we are able to follow the events which led up to his becoming a painter. Perhaps they may

SANTO *Hospital Hill:* The actual scene and the painting.

145

be regarded as a series of accidents, since the impetus generally came from others, but each painting attempt nevertheless reached a concluson gratifying to Santo.

His first association with art came as a little boy in Corsano where he watched the artists who were brought in from Naples to restore and "add saints and angels" to the church paintings. Santo recalls standing for hours at a time watching them. He tagged after artists just as boys here follow fire engines, but he had no desire to emulate them.

His first effort came many years later in Bennington. He was a house-painter at the time, and while painting a shoe repair shop for a friend, was asked to decorate a screen. The screen was to be painted anyway, so "why not make a picture on it" at the same time? The request came naturally from the proprietor and was accepted naturally by Santo. Here was a man who wanted a screen decorated; here a man with paints and brushes. The transition from painting a house to painting a picture was not an esthetic one; it was simply economic. Santo painted a girl in a canoe in the moonlight for $5 and the delighted storekeeper then asked him to do a 3'x12' mural in the same genre.

His next endeavor was several years later when he painted a velvet pillow top at the request of a friend. Her sister had died and this was to be a memento. The woman was very pleased with it, and when several girls at the mill where he was working saw it, he received orders for more than two dozen of them. But Santo soon tired of this and did not paint again for many years.

Finally because he had large wall areas in his home, he painted three big landscapes on wallboard. He still did not think of himself as an artist. He was busy earning a living and raising a family, and fifteen years passed between his screen for the shop and his initial canvas. The circumstances under which this canvas was painted were again most casual.

A cousin made rugs which she generally entered in the Rutland State Fair. Mrs. Santo understood her to say that if you submitted a work of art, you got a ticket of admission for the whole week of the fair. In 1937, she persuaded Santo to paint a picture which he sent along with a quilt Mrs. Santo's mother had made. When they visited the fair, they found they had to pay admission anyway, but there was a sequel to this incident, for the quilt won 2nd prize and Santo's painting was awarded 1st prize. Through this episode Santo began his career as an artist, for Walt Kuhn saw the prize-winning picture and sent a telegram to him asking if he had any more paintings. Santo had none. Kuhn then urged him to continue to paint but refrained from interfering with his talent, advising him only to use the best materials and telling him where to buy them. He had previously bought paints that were stale at a drugstore; yet they were the only ones he could obtain in town.

Santo's fortunate experiences were to continue. In 1938 three Santos were shown at the Southern Vermont Artists' Association in Manchester, where a picture was sold. In 1939, three of his works were included in the exhibition of *Unknowns* at the Museum of Modern Art. Not many months later, he was to enjoy a huge success. His first one-man show was held at Marie Harriman Galleries in the Spring of 1940, and thirty-three of the forty-seven paintings exhibited were sold. When asked about his reaction to all this, he replied:

I am more than satisfied with results obtained for my past efforts. They are far above my expectations but not to the point of self-satisfaction. They have only fired my ambitions to work harder and see just what I can do. Realism I think describes my attitude toward life and also toward art.

Winter Evening

WINTER EVENING, a quiet Vermont scene, is immaculately painted. The theme is a play of contrasts of pattern, of light and dark tonalities, of warm and cold values. Patterns in the snow, rocks, clouds, branches, and across the hilltops all engage each other to make these contrasts and oppositions.

The large fossil-like rock dominates the foreground, and immediately adjacent to its rigid bulk are placed softly bowing sprigs. Their delicacy and lightness and warm ochre color suggest early life, while the rock is age-old and is colder than even the surrounding snows.

The grey-barked tree in the foreground at the left and the white birch directly behind it form another variation and their branches spread and counterplay and overlap other branches of other trees, all of which makes a tracery across the sky. The clouds, reflecting the tawny tones of a setting sun, move on a plane between the interlacing branches and the cold blue sky.

Snow sharply isolates the rocks, shrubs and trees, whereas delicate shadings across the snow create a drift which makes a unit of them in the landscape.

Contrary to the usual procedure, Santo creates deep space by progression rather than recession, as in all his paintings he establishes his background first and then works forward. This is the way he gets the feel of spatial relationships. In this picture he began with the blue of the sky, painted the clouds against it, and then put in the rolling hills. Advancing step by step through the landscape, he reached the foremost tree and finally, close up, the huge rock.

Working as he does, he attains an intensity of form and a veracity of statement which he could not otherwise reach. For example, when working his sky and clouds, he made them his immediate problem and therefore wrought them with full concentration. Having set a high standard, he must at least sustain if not surpass it as he progresses forward where the demands are inevitably more exacting.

In the foreground perhaps a dramatic way to see this progression work is to note a segment of the dappled markings on the white bark of the birch. This fragment is magnified and restated in the snow-covered pyramidal rock which stands directly in front of it. A segment of this pattern is again enlarged and brought up in sharp focus in the huge rock in the foreground. We experience through Santo's advancing images a movement not unlike that of advancing cinematic shots.

In spite of its being predominantly a snow picture it is colorful, especially in the skies, where we have already noted the tawny brown and icy blue color gradations moving back and forth. Unfortunately these are lost in the reproduction since they are of equal photographic color value. Hemlock greens, and greys ranging through pearl, steel, mouse, and mauve are interspersed throughout the ivory and blue white snows.

Gliding clouds, reaching branches, rolling hills, bending sprigs, the drift of the snow, all these and the advancing planes give pulse to this quiet Vermont landscape.

148

TO   *Winter Evening.* 1940

MAX REYHER and his painting, *Wailing Wall*

CHAPTER TWELVE

MAX REYHER

ON THE winter's day that Max Reyher's granddaughter drove me out to visit him in Belmar, the rain froze as it fell and the roads were covered with a film of ice. We skidded half way across New Jersey. Arriving at last, we were welcomed by two elderly people, one of whom became most talkative, while the other attempted to hold him in check. Reyher, whose paintings are based on "themes," had so much to say about them, that once started, he was unable to stop. As Anita Brenner, who suggested his name, told me, his life has been so full of interests and hobbies, that he is overflowing with experiences. This is a factual account of his busy career:

150

Max Reyher was born in Berlin, Germany, June 1st, 1862. He studied at the Friedrichstädtische Gymnasium, learning the construction of mathematical instruments: microscope, telescope, spectroscope. For one year he studied optics at the University of Heidelberg, and in 1882 emigrated to the United States, settling in Philadelphia, where he became an optician. He retired in 1921 to pursue independently the study of entomology. He became a member of the Academy of Natural Science in Philadelphia, and formed a noted butterfly collection with specimens from all over the world. A part of this collection was eventually given to the Academy.

Each year Reyher raises thousands of butterflies for scientific experimentation and exchange. At the mating season, he ties the Queen butterfly to a tree by a long string so as not to lose it. By evening, he claims, male butterflies come from as far away as fifty miles in answer to signals sent by the antenna of the Queen. To feed his butterflies, he and his helper often walk twenty miles in search of proper leaves for their diet.

There are many passages in Reyher's paintings which remind one of the markings and colors on the wings of butterflies, and this gives to his work a very personal sense of pattern.

In the early '20's, he traveled extensively on the Continent and while visiting the great museums, he began to think for the first time about making pictures himself. The first painting he made was in 1926, a decoration for Mrs. Reyher's "hope-chest." It is folk-art and consists of a series of panels called *The Philosophy of Life*.

Of his work, he writes:

I have my own process for mixing colors, learning from the perfect coloring of butterflies. I call this "life-everlasting paint." I paint only on wood, and once applied, the paint dries instantaneously. I always make my own frames to suit the picture.

My object was to have thoughts behind every picture. I think the greatest artist in the world is Nature. The closer we come to Her, the greater artists we are. To paint of your own free will (if you have to, that is different) you must have inspiration. Otherwise it is mechanical.

About ten years ago three of his works were hung at the Weyhe Gallery, his only public showing.

He likes to philosophize about life and one of his favorite utterances is: "Life is motion. Lacking motion we have death." The titles he has given his

151

pictures reflect his inclination towards a religious, poetic mysticism. Some of them are:

Fairy Tale of the Spanish Moss   *The Last Human*
Act of Mercy   *The Spirit of Monte Carlo*
The Wailing Wall   *The Fairy Tale of the Nine Roses*
The Mystery   *The Flower's Revenge*
Christ Raising the Daughter of Jairus *The White Heron*

and *Nirwana*, a discussion of which follows.

Nirwana

TODAY I sent you a Poem by Ernst Eckstein in the German language. The poem is beautiful and very deep. I received the inspiration from it to paint *Nirwana*.

>*And lonely sounds in the endless space,*
>*The Song of everlasting dead.*

The *Nirwana* picture is freedom from all condition of existence. Nirwana is the shore of salvation for those who are in danger of being drowned in life's confusion.

Painted in 1928, *Nirwana* is Reyher's first easel picture. It is an *Isle of the Dead* picture in the same mystic spirit as that of Böcklin, the 19th century German painter. Böcklin's picture is drowned in the gloom of his own dark and muddy pigment, but Reyher's mysticism emerges through luminous enamel-like colors.

In the center of the painting is a huge diabolical rock which takes on the form of a death mask. Its eye is an empty space colored by the sky beyond. Across the stygian waters, a figure plunges in self-destruction over the cliff into the open jaws of death.

The isle behind the mask is a land of precipitous peaks and verdant growth permeated by a lavender pallor. Its crags are streaked with reflected light from the blood-red sun. The configuration of the melting sun upon the cloud is reminiscent of the image of Christ upon the kerchief.

White clouds, like ghosts of huge birds, hover in the sky, and hovering too is a dark cloud—the vulture.

152

REYHER   *Nirwana.* 1928   Collection Ferdinand Reyher, Hollywood.

BERNARD FROUCHTBEN at work on *My Ideal.*

CHAPTER THIRTEEN

BERNARD FROUCHTBEN

I HEARD of a tailor who was an amateur photographer reputed to have an unusually imaginative quality in his work. When I got to his shop I found him pressing—not clothes but photographs which he was mounting. Many of them were fresh and interesting, and as he warmed to my enthusiasm, he

154

showed me clippings of reproductions of his work. In the rotogravure section of an old issue of the Sunday *Forward*, a Yiddish language newspaper, was one of his amateur photographs and next to it, the reproduction of an amateur painting by someone else, which struck me as being very good. The picture was painted by a Bernard Frouchtben, and deciding to try to locate him, I made a note of the name, the date and the page.

The *Forward* after some delay informed me that they could not obtain the artist's address. I wrote an ad to appear in the following Sunday's edition, but before it was printed they had dug up an address for me. More than a month after I had written to that address, I received a telephone call, and it was Frouchtben. My letter had arrived, covered with forwarding addresses; it seemed Frouchtben moved around a lot. He now lives in the upper Bronx, where I visited him. A letter from him, quoted here in part, tells us his story:

I was born in 1872 in a little town in Southern Russia. As far as I remember I think I was born with a pencil in my hand. I remember being scolded by my mother for buying different colored crayon pencils with the few pennies I had. She couldn't understand a child who had his whole mind only on pencils. So I kept on scribbling and drawing all kinds of pictures throughout childhood.

Until one day a neighboring boy who went away to Odessa and attended a trade school there—cabinet making and drawing—returned and made my acquaintance. Subsequently he induced me to go with him to Paris to study art. By the way, this youth took me under his care and taught me his knowledge of cabinet work.

In 1890 we landed in Paris. We began work at cabinet making but at night I attended the school *Art et Metier* (Art & Craft) where I was taught the fundamentals of interior decorating. At the same time, with home study and attending other schools I received my education and knowledge.

At the earliest moment, with my first savings I purchased a box of paints and brushes and started to paint. I visited the art galleries, museums, in fact anything pertaining to painting.

But it seems that I picked up very well in art decoration and I made many original creations in furniture and interior work. So, little by little I made my own factory of reproductions of antiques and creations of French periods. Then I was in my right element. I had to do modeling, bronzes, wood carving, marquetry, and painting for decoration on furniture. In spare time, as a hobby, I still kept on going with my canvas painting, my first love, never expecting to have any material gains of it but happy when I could accomplish something.

For a long period the factory was successful. I established a big name in the field. But it grew too large to handle and profits began to disappear as it was too much art for the market. In the meantime I was married. With business going bad I was open

155

to suggestion. I was told that in America I could be very successful with my capabilities in this type of craftsmanship as money was plentiful and people were ready to spend freely. In fact I had customers from the United States.

So in 1908 I landed in New York with my wife. The little money we had with us went rapidly without opening a factory. In the meantime a little girl was born and I found a job in a factory as a cabinet maker. I was there seven years and had nothing but wages. Meantime I made up my mind to learn architecture, thinking that it would be a better livelihood. I attended Cooper Union and at the same time took up a course in the International Correspondence School on architecture. But in the long run I realized there was no future in it either. As far as success was concerned it would be just as difficult as with my paintings.

Eventually I was able to establish a factory for making reproductions of French period furniture adapted to American life. At the beginning I was successful till they started to copy my work and made it much cheaper than I could produce it. Then I went into the business of importing carved furniture from Europe. That necessitated bi-yearly trips to Europe covering France, Italy, Belgium and England. But keeping step with me was my shadow of painting. In traveling I picked up several inspirations and notions that I transferred to canvases. But with all my art work I never expected any material benefits from it. I looked at it as a very pitiable state when anyone offered me a little something just to have a hand painting. But I was happy to give my paintings to anyone whom I knew liked and appreciated them.

In 1929-1930 I lost all my money and my business. At the same time I fell sick. By that time my daughter was married and I had already a grandchild. I couldn't work any more—my whole time was spent in painting. As my wife didn't like the situation we separated. The idea of having an artist husband without any money was distasteful to her. Of course that meant the breaking up of the home and I landed in a furnished room. Then, just walking around in the park and transmitting my feelings and ideas, I made my first self-portrait presenting a figure of myself unemployed. But then I thought, I *am* employed, I am painting.

As it happened, I was in the *Forward* building and stopped in to see Mr. Kahn with the thought of making some sort of financial use of my paintings. I showed him my work, claiming that when the *Forward* was small I was instrumental in aiding its growth. Liking my work, claiming that for no one would he do the same, but my work being outstanding, he gave me that quarter page space for the printing of my picture which picture you saw in the paper.

Every morning as usual I take my walk through the isolated alleys of the upper Bronx. It impressed me looking at the forlorn alleys with their bare trees deprived of their glorious leaves with only a few yellow leaves left which the wind couldn't tear off, that not so long ago I remembered them so glorious and bright and green, forming a big shadow protecting people from the sun's rays, crowded with people underneath them looking for rest and coolness under their shadow—now they looked lonely and sad—their yellow leaves lying on the ground covering the earth like a golden frock, beautiful anyhow, till the wind and the rain will wash them away. Often it came in my mind, "does it make any difference to human beings?" One is fresh and healthy,

156

full of life, everything is hopeful and prosperous, then the autumn of life comes and everything little by little seeps away. Children grow up and become occupied with their own lives, ambitions, emotions, friends, and own plans for the future, leaving the parent isolated and alone.

What? Am I an exception, the only one? It is the human, natural way of the evolution of society and millions of people are affected that way. And maybe because through the generations it is that way we have to console ourselves as a fact that it is so. It often came in my mind to illustrate this point on canvas and that is one of the factors for *Lonely Man on a Lonely Road*, which you found in my place and I am happy you liked.

That is all I can tell you—*facts without literature.*

Lonely Man on a Lonely Road

THIS IS the painting about which Frouchtben wrote so touchingly in his letter. The lone figure walking down the road is, as he has written, a self-portrait. Over the picture is an air of isolation, of enclosure, of introspection. Barricaded by the rows of trees which arch over him, he is shut in upon the long road where he wanders alone. There is no welcome in the houses along the way. On the contrary, the fiery red brick house in the foreground is walled in, its gates are closed, and its two green windows peer at him suspiciously over the parapet, as if they were the glassy eyes of some obsessed creature, watching his every move.

Painted on a wooden panel in warm autumn browns, the complex pattern of gnarled branches is flecked with rusty leaves. The mottled, light-filled, grey blue clouds descend to the horizon where the color deepens to blue, and, merging with the greens of the distant landscape, filters through the maze of trees in peacock colors.

The road has a rich patina of mellow golden earth colors which brighten as it recedes. To the exclusion of the sombre world about the figure, a flicker of light plays upon the road, as if it were illuminated from some other source than the sun, and this gives the impression that the man is walking in a halo of light.

In composition and subject matter the painting is remarkably similar to Valdes' *Cuban Landscape*. Both have long receding roads lined with trees whose branches close in over the single figure in the foreground. The road of each is bathed in a strange glow from a mysterious source that is unrelated to the familiar light which falls upon the rest of the picture. Valdes' lonely man, like Frouchtben's, is poignantly felt.

The idea of compositional arrangement which involves a receding plane in the center of the picture is one often used by self-taught painters. Through the book one will find several compositions of a similar nature. Besides Frouchtben and Valdes, there are Litwak (*Fifth Avenue*), Hirshfield (*Beach Girl*), and Samet (*Cell Interior*). The desire to achieve a deep recession of space is usually given by the artist as his motive; but in all probability he is trying just to express his loneliness. That all these paintings are bi-symmetrically planned is not necessarily of psychological significance, but is rather an elementary pictorial idea.

LICHTBEN   *Lonely Man on a Lonely Road.* 1936

CHARLES HUTSON on his 94th birthday. 1934

CHAPTER FOURTEEN

CHARLES HUTSON

CHARLES WOODWARD HUTSON was born in 1840 in McPhersonville, S. C. His ancestors on both sides were Colonial settlers. He was a man of letters, of wide experience in life and culture. His flow of creative energy, continuous all his life, brought him at the age of sixty-five to painting. While such an age is almost the end for many, for Hutson it was but a new beginning, for he was to paint steadily for thirty years to the end of his long and full life.

160

His daughter, Ethel Hutson, writes a most understanding letter about him, appraising her father's creative achievements with rare critical ability. Because of the significance of what she says, it is quoted here out of its context:

Writing was the most natural form of expression for him. Essays, novels, verse, letters all poured from his pen with amazing facility. Yet with a few rare exceptions, his writing showed less originality and creative force than did his painting. Perhaps the slight barrier of the unfamiliar medium of painting dammed the flow of his creative power just enough to give the impetus his facile writing seemed often to lack.

Here is Charles Hutson from his own reminiscences and as seen by his daughter:

. . . I have been reading over the little Ms called *My Reminiscences* which my father wrote at various intervals during the latter years of his life. It was written, not for publication, but for his children and grandchildren. In it he covers his long life very sketchily, telling of various events and his many moves from place to place in the years when every Southern school or college had a hard struggle to keep going, and pay even a part of the meager salaries promised to its teachers. The outstanding impression one gets is that in spite of poverty, reverses, disappointments, even the loss of loved ones, he kept his serene faith, his love of God and man, his joy in nature and in all things beautiful, in art and letters particularly.

. . . Though he records the battles in the War of Secession in which he took part, was wounded and a prisoner for three bitter months in Fort Delaware, these same pages are full of comments on the kindnesses shown him and other soldiers by the folk of the country through which they passed, the beauty of the scenery.

. . . He often declared that he had been "only an amateur" all his life in all his varied occupations. Enlisting in the Confederate army as a private just after his graduation from the S. C. College, he was, he pointed out, "an amateur soldier," though he studied for the legal profession and was duly admitted to the bar, the economic and social conditions of the post-war period prevented him from becoming a professional lawyer, and he became, without any special training for the job, "an amateur teacher." All his life he wrote, and published much, but most of it in short-lived publications which seldom paid! So he could call himself "only an amateur writer." Finally, entering on the experiment of painting at the age of 65, he never claimed professional competence in that field, always insisting on that even when he had been practicing painting for 30 years! I believe he did succeed in keeping the spirit of the amateur—the "lover"—in all he did, and that is why his work gives joy to others.

Though he had a Presbyterian distaste for symbolism or the use of emblems, it is curious to note that his work became more and more symbolic, more and more mystical. Toward the last he seemed to see colors and forms that were not visible to other eyes—particularly a certain marvellous "blue" which he tried in vain to put into his pictures. He would try every sort of blue pigment he could get, but none of them were right, he complained.

161

His wide reading and his remarkable memory for historic relations—not merely facts—made him an inspiring lecturer to his classes, and also gave him much subject matter for his painting. His delight in poetry and in fiction, both of which he read with joy and wrote with fluency, were akin to his love of trees and flowers, sea and shore. All these factors entered into his art when he began to paint, for the images stored up in his mind during a life-time of living in varied environments, from his native South Carolina "low country" to the mountains of Virginia and the plains of Texas made up the inner world in which he dwelt, more at home than in the world of everyday happenings. Yet he was scrupulous in the performance of any duty expected of him, from attending chapel in the colleges in which he taught, to doing the daily marketing for the family after we came to New Orleans, a task he greatly enjoyed for the contact it gave him with the humble market folk. He was never "Bohemian" in the sense of considering himself free to disregard ordinary obligations. Order, neatness, punctuality, and the courtesy of "noblesse oblige" were a part of his upbringing.

In his *Reminiscences* he says little of his painting, barely mentioning it as one of the ways he spent his time happily after his retirement from teaching.

. . . He often said that those who affected a scorn for "form" failed to realize that form was a vital factor in life as well as in art. "Even in the art of cooking," he would say at the breakfast-table, "you can see how the same batter, cooked as a waffle, a muffin, or a battercake becomes an entirely different thing." So in his painting he was always seeking a good composition of forms, a grouping of trees, roadway, sky or sea that satisfied him.

. . . Though he was not "naive," or uncultivated, nor child*ish*, he was to the end of his life singularly child*like*, simple-hearted, full of fresh wonder at nature, life and the world. I think that is why his work still gives joy to others.

When Hutson was 91, his first one-man show was held at the Isaac Delgado Museum of Art, New Orleans, where 47 oils were exhibited. He died in New Orleans four years later in 1935. His champions in New York include Claire Hopkins to whom the above letter was written, Joseph Solmon, artist, and J. B. Neumann, art dealer and lecturer, who has recently presented a one-man show of his work in New York.

162

Carnival in Royal Street

CARNIVAL IN ROYAL STREET expresses the hilarity of the Mardi Gras. The artist who lived for so many years among these people has caught the high spirits of the event.

The flaming torch carried by the huge burnt-cork clown in the foreground is the insignia of the carnival and the high color note in the picture. It plays upon the people who move and dance across the picture, catching the color of their costumes, and throws an eerie light upon the buildings in the background.

There are no garlands or banners upon the facades to make the occasion more gala. But the people standing behind the grillwork on the balconies, their costumes in the half-light echoing the gay colors of the paraders, become a series of decorative patterns festooning the buildings.

The forward surge of the procession is the dominating movement of the picture, and all the other movement is subtly oriented to this. Led by two elderly people prancing in stately fashion, come the revelers, embracing or dancing alone, in twos or fours. Whatever gay bit of performing animates them, the general impetus of the procession is forward. Advancing in scale as they approach, all of the parading figures move between the line of the curb and the bottom of the balconies on the houses. In this reserved area they are given full right-of-way, with no architectural obstructions of any kind to impede their progress.

As the general axis of the merry-makers is forward, the tendency of the houses is to lean backward. The buildings, slightly awry, form a counter-movement to the procession, receding like a moving train. Psychologically, this heightens the tempo of the parade.

We have seen that no architectural details interfere with or offer resistance to the marchers, and that they move freely within their own path. In Litwak's *Fifth Avenue* (p. 143) we find figures placed similarly in relation to architecture, that is, without any overlapping. But it is interesting to see how this result in both pictures was achieved from quite opposite approaches. With Litwak this was an elemental way of reasoning, whereas with Hut-

163

son we find that it is a plastic preference and a sensitive way of establishing kinetics, since he does not avoid this overlapping throughout the picture but only where freedom of movement is essential. Even here, while the figures have complete access to the space within which they move, they overlap each other in a complex arrangement of plane upon plane. In addition, the huge clown is superimposed on the background of figures and buildings; and the watchers on the balconies of course are seen *through* the grillwork. Clearly, then, Hutson's device of keeping the paraders within a free space was one of *choice*, even though perhaps intuitive, rather than of elemental concept.

The overlarge figure of the clown logically fits into this scheme of visual movement, but only through his exaggerated size, for beset with resistance by the buildings and the marchers, he is able only through sheer bulk to keep up with the parade. He is like a giant marionette symbolizing the nocturnal festivities.

The oil color is dry and has the quality of thickly applied pastel. The varied tonalities and gradations are as knowing as Degas', but are set down with the emotional spontaneity of a child, yet with the technical assurance of the Expressionist Painters. The apparently sketchy painting of the animated figures manages to express the mood and the movement of each. While the forms are not sharply defined, neither are they vague, for the conception is definite and the statement positive. The expressionist technique, in fact, is perfectly suited emotionally and pictorially to the picture's content.

The Queen of the carnival is the fifth figure in the parade, and homage is paid to her obliquely by a canopy or arch inadvertently formed by people. On the balcony above her crowned head stands a lone figure with outstretched arms. The lines of these arms form the apex of the arch. Extended on one side, the line is caught by the slant of the woman leading the march; on the other by the raised arm of the dancing girl in the center.

At this point the gestures along the march build up to a climax and the crossed arms of the two girls become the X that marks the spot.

164

ɪʀSON *Carnival in Royal Street.*   Collection J. B. Neumann.

CHAPTER FIFTEEN

WILLIAM SAMET

LITTLE MATERIAL is available on William Samet. He was born in Astoria, L. I., in 1908 and is a prison artist—an inmate at Dannemora where he is serving a life sentence. His prison occupation is that of a metal worker, and easel painting is an optional interest.

The first opportunity I had of seeing his work was at the Independent show in New York in 1936, where his *Prison Yard* was exhibited. His next public showing was in 1939 when both *Prison Yard* and *Cell Interior: Artist at Easel*, the latter reproduced here, were seen at the *Unknowns* exhibition at the Museum of Modern Art.

The painting reproduced on page 169 exists in photograph only, and the following description is from notes taken when it was in New York in 1939:

Cell Interior: Artist at Easel

Cell Interior is a penetrating portrait of the *Artist at Easel*. Receding perspectives enclosing the lone figure make it the same basic composition as Valdes' *Cuban Landscape* and Frouchtben's *Lonely Man*. The enclosure in the two latter pictures is subjective alone; here it is both subjective and factual.

If the painter and his easel were lifted out of their environment, the unit would represent the usual artist working concentratedly upon his canvas, a portrait of a young girl. Emotional significance appears not in the self portrait but in the surroundings. The figure is walled in by metal-colored brick and recurring throughout the painting are disconsolate and jaundiced areas of mustard browns and wan yellows. His sun is an electric bulb. The agonized handling of drapes and clothing on the wall are definite subconscious reflections. The formidable bars across the cell opening have been softened by curtains, but with the environment closing in on all sides, the feeling of confinement is intense.

The small cut at the chapter head is the only current portrait of the artist available. It is a detail of the repainted version of his *Cell Interior* of 1936. The two portraits reproduced here are separated by an interval of only four years, and a comparison between them, as well as the subject matter on the easel, is revealing.

WILLIAM SAMET   Detail of 1940 version, *Cell Interior: Artist at Easel.*

168

MET   *Cell Interior: Artist at Easel.* 1936

169

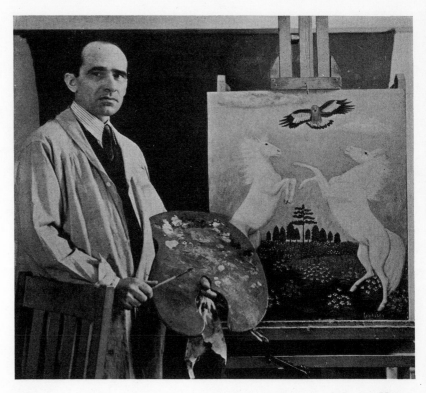

LAWRENCE LEBDUSKA and *Circus Horses.*

CHAPTER SIXTEEN

LAWRENCE LEBDUSKA

LAWRENCE LEBDUSKA was born in Baltimore, in 1894. His father, a Bo-
hemian stained-glass worker, had been sent there by the Leipzig firm of
Fleider & Schneider. When Lawrence was five, his parents returned to
Europe, taking him with them.

170

He was educated in Leipzig, eventually learning the stained-glass craft at a technical school run by the same firm. Later, in an international art exhibition there, he won a prize for his painting *Bit of Bohemia*. In the meantime he had also studied decorating under Joseph Svoboda in Chrudim, Bohemia.

Lebduska returned to America at the age of eighteen. His first job in New York City was with Elsie de Wolfe, for whom he did wall decorations. After three seasons with her, he entered upon a career of his own as a decorator. In his spare time, he continued painting easel pictures.

The initial public appearance of his paintings was at the Opportunity Gallery of the Art Centre in 56th Street, where Louis Kaufman, the violinist, purchased the first of the many Lebduska oils now in his collection in Hollywood. Lebduska continued to exhibit at the Art Centre for three years, until it closed its doors in 1929, and it was during this time that I first saw his paintings. His work was later shown at the Bourgeois Gallery, and a small group was exhibited at the 8th Street Playhouse in 1935. In 1936, the artist had a large one-man show at the Contemporary Art Galleries in 54th Street, and has since had other one-man exhibits at 57th Street galleries. He has also been employed on the WPA Art Project in New York.

Animals constitute the subject matter for the greater part of Lebduska's work. They are usually brightly painted and vari-colored. Lebduska once lived with an uncle who breeds horses in Orangeville, Md., where he had ample opportunity to observe these animals in all their tempers. He also researches at zoos and at the American Museum of Natural History, but prefers to read books describing animals' color, forms, and habits. His observations lead not to reality, but to a world of folk-fantasy.

The Flood

IN *The Flood* by Lebduska, the rushing waters eddy and swirl and the excitement is picked up by the clouds which are whipped about in the storm. The turmoil being the same in water and sky, with only a faint line of demarcation between them, there is a feeling of rising waters filling the picture. The fury of the storm is heightened by the spreading branches which crackle across the clouds like flashes of lightning. One of the lower branches has broken off, and, protruding from the water, is like a groping claw futilely clutching at space.

Although the houses remain firmly planted, confusion and havoc are strongly suggested in the handling of colors which are so intense and boldly juxtaposed that they appear almost chaotic. This is effective in that it acts as a series of color contrasts such as olive green and red orange trim, salmon beige with blue green trim and brick red chimneys. The auto which is partly submerged in sea green waters, is bright red with yellow stripes and orange fenders.

In contrast to his other pictures which are generally thinly painted, Lebduska has added power to his statement here where it is needed by sheer use of paint heavily applied with a palette knife.

Sympathy is created by the plight of the people, the man as lookout, the girl lashed to the trunk, the little dog on a leash, awaiting their impending rescue.

ꜱᴋᴀ *The Flood.* 1934. Collection M. Martin Janis, Buffalo.

ELLA SOUTHWORTH and her paintings against a "Belgian Panel.

CHAPTER SEVENTEEN

ELLA SOUTHWORTH

ONE DAY my wife and I went "antiquing" for early American paintings and found instead late American paintings at a "museum" in Essex, Conn. It was a tiny antique shop, to which a friend, Freddy Lake, had sent us, and in a rear room we were assailed by a barrage of bright canvases. After some questioning the proprietor told us they were painted by "Sis." We remained for a time enjoying them and presently a tall, elderly woman

174

entered the room with a gingery step. She was "Sis," the proprietor's wife. I inquired: "Are you the artist?" and she replied: "Don't call me an artist, I am a *painter*." She had won the day.

Long afterward, she wrote this account of her life:

I was born in Westbrook, Conn. Jan. 11th, 1872. My father followed the sea, until he yielded to my mother's insistence that he stay on land, so after their marriage he became a house painter, gradually taking up the finer lines until he was doing fresco work in churches and so on. He had a most wonderful idea of color and a most excellent taste for design. I always had free access to his workshop where I used to decorate the walls with all sorts of pictures, ladies in wonderful gowns, trees, houses and all sorts of things. From this, I began to paint pictures when about 12 years old just from sheer love of creating things in paint. I kept on painting at intervals giving away my work but always loving it, until my marriage in 1905 when I gave it up and for 25 years I never touched a brush.

All at once the urge to paint returned and I began all over again, ten years ago. I'll never stop again. I've been a dressmaker, a hairdresser, and a laundress, but I'll always be a painter from now on.

The following are brief quotations from her many lovely letters:

I like to do all kinds of pictures as it is a pleasure to go from one to the other. Flowers too. This is where the diversion comes and when a little scene develops like a jewel, then I'm glad I didn't try to do a great big thing.

I am having "all the fun" for it is no effort for me to paint. In fact it is recreation. When I am very tired after doing my other work I can sit down and take my brushes and forget all about it. It's like going away somewhere on a vacation.

Yesterday I received your letter saying that all three paintings were accepted for the *Unknown American Painters* show and this morning's mail brought the letter from the Museum of Modern Art. This is such a chapter of happenings that it is pretty breath-taking. To think after all these years of fighting along with almost no recognition at all, that I should at last arrive in such a wonderful manner. To demonstrate my gratitude to you, I will try to paint worthily.

I have not been doing very much at pictures for about three weeks. But—I have been painting just the same. I've painted the kitchen chairs, the water pump, the step-on can, and the outside of the kitchen sink, a combination of jade green and dove grey.

In November I began to get ready for the holidays which mean so much to us. First 'twas Thanksgiving then the first of December, a birthday dinner to my only brother, which took much thought and planning. Then I began doing things for Christmas and I've knitted four sweaters besides doing lots of other things. All this time my laundry has been going full speed. New Year's came along and you know, that day is something more than just another day to my husband and me. This one was the 35th anniversary of our marriage.

175

Filled to brimming with local relics, the Southworths' "Riverview Museum" is a diminutive historical society. It is never left alone for long, and if one or the other does go off to visit a neighbor, he is seldom beyond earshot and can be readily summoned by a call blown from a conch-shell.

Golden Thoughts

THE OPINION that a painting is a self-portrait regardless of subject matter has validity in that some part of the artist inevitably remains within the work. In *Golden Thoughts* we find a great deal of Ella Southworth. It is a tender idea audaciously presented; it is gay yet pensive.

A bowl of delicate pansies nurtured and gathered by her from her own garden is pithily painted in vigorous colors. We think of cream whites, butter cup yellows and burnished golds as sensitive colors; and of pansies as fragile flowers. Here, in a bowl of electric blue, they are set down in no mincing terms. Still the pansies have lost none of their airy character—they tumble around and out of the bowl with fresh gaiety. This activity is accompanied by the scalloped pattern on the bowl. It is echoed by the shape of the doily, and reverberates throughout the dark wallpaper across the background.

The placing of the still-life mass in relation to the rectangle of the canvas is courageous. Equally courageous is the way the canvas cuts off the table-top on one side and the seascape picture hanging on the wall, on the other. The table-top and the wall picture are counterpoised and the single corner of each which is in view creates a tension between them. By this means they keep each other from sailing out of the picture and hold the complex pattern-upon-pattern securely in place.

HAZEL KNAPP and her m

CHAPTER EIGHTEEN

HAZEL KNAPP

HAZEL KNAPP, long an invalid, used to paint her landscapes from her wheel chair. If a bend in the road, or a tree, obscured her view, her mother would go directly to the scene and from this vantage point, sometimes the side of a mountain, report back to Hazel the details that lay beyond her field of vision.

178

These would be incorporated in the painting—a cooperative venture, Mrs. Knapp furnishing the eyes which enabled her daughter to see around corners.

One might imagine from this that her pictures contain conflicting viewpoints, but such is not the case. Her faithful, understanding mother was able to give just the right degree of assistance, and the work remains personal.

Hazel, who is in the early thirties, started to draw as a child, and has continued ever since. Her physical handicap and consequent enforced idleness may have given her the opportunity for constant drawing and the possibility of effecting a natural transition to adult painting. She works in water-color and if she feels the picture is "worth-while," makes a larger oil of it. Her water-colors are more spontaneous, but in her oils there is a ripening which gives them substance.

In 1932 she entered her first oil in the Southern Vermont Artists' Association exhibition. This picture was sold and the following Christmas Hazel received a gift of a complete set of paints. In 1933 at the same annual exhibition Alfred Harcourt, the publisher, bought a snow picture. The following year when Harcourt-Brace published the American edition of Gertrude Stein's *The Making of Americans*, Miss Stein came over from Paris, and on a visit to Mr. Harcourt saw the painting. Impressed, she wired to Hazel in Vermont asking to see more of her work. Hazel had none ready, but painting best under pressure—she has the vitality and zest for such a situation—turned out four canvases that week and sent them to New York. When last heard of, these canvases were in Paris—Gertrude Stein had bought all four of them. Miss Stein is understood to have arranged for an exhibition of Hazel's work, together with other "primitive" Vermont painters which was to have been held in Paris in November of 1939. Of course the war intervened.

I was introduced to Hazel's paintings by Harriette Miller, the artist, who looks after her like a godmother, and is very sympathetic to her work. In 1939 at the *Unknowns* exhibition a sparkling *Snow Scene* was included.

When we visited Hazel in 1941, she was no longer an invalid. She told

179

us Mrs. Miller had sent her to a New York doctor. For the first time in all these years she is now able to walk.

Guardians of the Valley

OUR INTRODUCTION to *Guardians of the Valley* is really via the younger generation of "guardians," for, in an oblique row, they lead us into the composition. After the formalities of meeting their elders—the true Guardians, we proceed further by rolling down in rapid succession the three snow covered hills directly behind. From here our course zig-zags across the valley and up and up to the mountain tops, very much as a sailboat tacking interminably against strong winds.

Painted in tones of icy blues, wintry greys and sleet whites to the exclusion of all other colors, its frigidity is intensified. The valley lying in the mountains, stretches across the center of the canvas like a huge hammock supported on either side by snow-laden hemlocks, the Guardians. Directly above the top of each of these are frost-encrusted branches of nearby trees which seem to form a hood of crackling ice. By way of a humorous commentary on Vermont winter, the evergreens are capped with frozen hoods as if better to stand the long siege of winter.

APP *Guardians of the Valley.* 1938

CHAPTER NINETEEN

RENAULT TOURNEUR

TOURNEUR PROMISED to write a short account of his life, and when he sent
it on—a fabulous story—he penned this postscript:

I never aspired to the knack of writing, but does it seem fair to expect coherence
and lucidity in a compressed mass of 90 years of eventful experiences in the same
space given youngsters of fifty? I sketched 1500 words, on counting, find it 3000. I
resketched so as to condense, count again and find 4500. So what's the use. Wish I
could grow crops that way. I'd return to the farm. . . .

According to Tourneur, his parents were killed when he was an infant.
This happened in 1851 in what was then known as Texas-Louisiana country. He was reared by Comanche Indians.

I was but a Comanche papoose en passage to a strange country.
. . . I ceased to lead an unsuccessful planned orderly life and just got busy doing
the things I was prompted to do, and quit only by outgrowing them or becoming
enticed in some other energy outlet. . . .
Most of my adventures in the supposedly unknown, were found to be some un-
finished jobs or at least aspirations of some of my ancestors. . . . That leads me to
assert that such claims as spurts of genius often at a late date in life are but some
ancestral skill or consuming aspirations breaking through. Their delay in asserting
themselves being mainly due to lack of openings to enter, through experience or
through its vicarious pal, Education. Many avenues of approach to that part of us
that keeps the machinery agoing is cleared of accumulated rubbish, and unsuspected
talent appears. . . .
To recount my own experiences in most any line would just be to borrow pages out
of my ancestral logbook. Every credit is due my ancestors, the failures—mine. . . .
Most every picture I paint is so violent as to threaten decorum when shown beside
other pictures in a house or gallery. They are mostly turbulent seascapes or else the
equally disturbing scenes of the pale skins' unrelenting fiendish methods in exter-
minating the natives of the Western hemisphere. Being from infancy until a late date
among most of the then undisturbed natives from the Rio Grande to far into Canada
and east into the Ottawas, I am familiar with much of their then family and tribal
life, and have depicted it on skins, bark, lumber, and canvas, from small "souvenirs"
to expansive murals. Many were done on location, sketched while some important
historical action was taking place and when I knew nothing at all about painting except to apply home made colors the way they appeared to me. . . .

182

While yet a papoose I developed remarkable accuracy in line drawing, mostly on pottery, metal ornaments and in carving designs. Coloring I got from the rug weavers. This I picked up from many tribes, some of whom were our deadly enemies such as the Apache, Piutes, Hopi and Navajo. A papoose was never molested. . . . My greatest proficiency consisted in depicting narratives, heroic deeds and other tales in line drawing. At that time my main personal problem was to get rid of my loosening upper front baby teeth. . . .

His story continues, telling of fantastic adventures on land and at sea in many countries of the globe:

It was while a pirate captive that I got my first introduction to Indo-China and Chinese life and architecture, and incidentally that of Burma. The Moorish and Algerian complex I got while pinch hitting as a "Legion d' Estrangeur" in Morocco.

Almost all of these and plenty other radically different experiences in vocations, travels and contacts contribute toward a broadening of one's vision to be incorporated in paintings or rather the self-painted portrait of the artist. Many there are who specialize in a certain subject and make a good living thereat, but that is work, labor, a chore, no matter how well executed, and I see no fun therein. The pleasure is to do a job which, when finished, even startles, and makes me wonder wherefrom I got that stuff. The theme, the figures, the action, all taken out of the land of hallucinations, but lively, interesting, decorous and fascinating to the spectator—this is the purpose of a picture.

The foregoing biographical fragments appertain only to the starting of my part-time or avocational painting.

In 1939, I saw Tourneur's paintings for the first time in Washington Square. On Waverly Place, he set up his pictures somewhat apart from the rest. My younger son was with me. He had been studying various aspects of Indian life at school that year, and he became absorbed in Tourneur's Indian fantasies. He had little difficulty interpreting many of the symbols, and consequently the very young child and the very old man had a mutually delightful time in their world of Indian lore.

Recently Tourneur was engaged to paint about 600 square feet of murals in a bakery. These are now almost finished, and promise to be some of his most interesting work. One wall is "autobiographical"—epic in subject matter—and the others are filled with symbolic and decorative fantasy. The story-of-his-life, forty feet long, is filled with diminutive figures painted in the technique and scale of an easel picture.

The Siwanoy Night Patrol

THE LORE in this painting belongs perhaps more to the invention of the artist than to Indian legend. Tourneur has often spoken about his childhood with the Comanches, a Plains tribe, and his knowledge of the myths of other tribes, but there does not seem to exist a myth which corresponds to this picture.

The nude goddess and the multi-colored seashell are both unusual in Indian mythology. The whip of lightning which she wields represents the Thunder and is the Indian Foe of Water Monsters, although the three individually colored monsters here seem Oriental.

The goddess rides the shell as though it were a surfboard drawn by the water serpents which she is spurring on toward the rising sun like an Indian Aurora speeding the coming of the new day. With supernatural assurance she aquaplanes across the eddying waters whose crests break and swirl around her skiff.

There is a burst of brilliant color in the sky which softens as it lights upon the mysterious shores and catches the foaming waters. Venus-Aurora and her shell shine forth with the full glow of the rising sun, rivalling in splendor the coming of Dawn.

184

URNEUR   *The Siwanoy Night Patrol.*

185

HORACE PIPPIN painting *Woman of Samaria.*   Now in the Collection of the Barnes Foundation, Me

186

CHAPTER TWENTY

HORACE PIPPIN

OF PIPPIN's work, Dr. Albert C. Barnes wrote in 1940:

The refreshing novelty of Horace Pippin's paintings grows in substance and meaning as one progresses in the search for its cause; it becomes an abiding characteristic
when one finds convincing evidence that Pippin has had a fresh insight into Nature
and tells about it simply, directly, and in a language of his own. It is the language of
poetry, homely poetry with the charm, simplicity, sincerity and naïveté characteristic
of all authentic folk art. And, like its forebears, it has the individual savor of its soil:
Pippin's art is distinctly American; its ruggedness, vivid drama, stark simplicity, pic-
turesqueness, and accentuated rhythms, have their musical counterparts in the Spirit-
uals of the American Negro.

. . . To hold against Pippin his present inability to make pigment express his ideas
and feelings with refinement and finesse, is equivalent to finding fault with Andrew
Jackson because he never went to college.

The following are documentary excerpts from Pippin's autobiography:

187

MY LIFE'S STORY

By Horace Pippin

I were born in West Chester, Pa. on Feb. 22, 1888. In Goshen when I was seven I began to get into trouble. It happened this way. In spelling, if the word was dog, stone, dishpan or something like that, I had a sketch of the article at the end of the word. And the results were, I would have to stay in after school and finish my lesson the right way. This happened frequently.

One day I got a magazine with a lot of advertisements in it of dry goods. In it there were a sketch of a very funny face. Under this face printed in large letters, it said make me and win a prize. And I did and sent it to Chicago. The following week the prize came, it was a box of crayon pencils of six different colors. Also a box of cold water paint and two brushes. These I were delighted in and used them often.

. . . I got a yard of muslin and cut it into six pieces, then fringed the edge of each making a doily out of them. On each I drew a biblical picture. These I worked faithfully over using my colored crayon pencils and took them to the Sunday School festival. They were hung on a wire along the wall to be sold. . . . Later when I came in I looked along the wall where the doilies had been hung and they were missing. I asked my teacher what had happened to them. She told me they had been sold to an old lady. One day about a month after the festival, a lady standing in her door, stopped me, and asked me if I wasn't Horace Pippin, I answered yes mam. She asked me if I made the doilies. I told her yes. She said "You certainly make some bum things," and drew her hand from under her apron. In her hand was a clean piece of fringed muslin. She said "Look at this, I bought it at the festival with a picture on it. I washed it and this is all I have." I explained to her that the picture was only made of crayon and could not be washed.

At the age of fourteen I went to work on a farm. . . . I was now fifteen years old, and my first job was unloading coal at the coal yard. I went from the coal yard to a feed store, and from job to job, until I got a job as porter, and I was now eighteen. I was there for seven years.

Pippin entered the Army in July, 1917, and after a year of harrowing experiences in France, of which he gives a long and realistic account in his autobiography, was badly wounded, eventually returning to America in January, 1919, where he was honorably discharged from service. While in France he had made sketches:

My mind goes back to the sketches I had made in France, which I had to destroy. . . . I married in 1920 Nov. 25th. I started to make drawings on wood panels ten years after my discharge. Still my arm and shoulder were so weak I could not work long at a time, but I kept trying. One day I decided to get some oil paint, and I started the picture that was in my mind, The Ending of the War: Starting Home, and made others until my work was discovered by Dr. Christian Brinton. This is my life's story from 1888 to 1940.

188

Dr. Brinton arranged an exhibition of his work at the West Chester Community Center in 1937, and in 1938 three of Pippin's oils were included in the *Masters of Popular Painting* exhibition. He had one-man shows of oils and burntwood panels in 1940 and 1941 at the Carlen Galleries in Philadelphia, and during that season, he had an exhibition at the Bignou Gallery, New York, as well.

In the catalogue of the exhibition at the Museum of Modern Art in 1938, he is quoted as saying:

How I Paint: The colors are very simple such as brown, amber, yellow, black, white and green. The pictures which I have already painted come to me in my mind, and if to me it is a worth while picture, I paint it. I go over that picture in my mind several times and when I am ready to paint it I have all the details that I need. I take my time and examine every coat of paint carefully and to be sure that the exact color which I have in mind is satisfactory to me. Then I work my foreground from the background. That throws the background away from the foreground. In other words bringing out my work. The time it takes to make a picture depends on the nature of the picture. For instance the picture called *The Ending of the War: Starting Home* which was my first picture. On that picture I couldn't do what I really wanted to do, but my next pictures I am working my thought more perfectly. My opinion of art is that a man should have love for it, because my idea is that he paints from his heart and mind. To me it seems impossible for another to teach one of Art.

The End of the War: Starting Home

PIPPIN BEGAN *The End of the War: Starting Home,* his first oil, in 1930. Working laboriously on it for three years, he applied coat upon coat until the pigment on his forms stood out in relief.

Extremely low in color key, the dark greys, blackish olive greens, heavy khaki browns and predominating blacks form an abysmally bleak setting for the action.

The title to the contrary notwithstanding, it does not seem to be the end of the war, nor are the soldiers starting home. On the contrary the colored regiment of American soldiers is engaged in capturing Germans.

The introduction of deep red color notes intensifies the emotional impact of the picture for they act as signals of danger, either actual or impending. They appear in sudden bursts in the core of the exploding bombs spotting the sky just above the woods. They pour in flames from an enemy plane plummeting earthward. Red insignia on uniforms "earmark" the retreating and surrendering Boches. Finally the bloody helmet on the right tells of the dying "buddy" lying prone on the earth.

The forms in the picture, worked over until they were strongly stated, are accented by relief rather than by color. Today Pippin's color is no longer dark and foreboding. He knows how to work in brighter color and need no longer struggle as he did in the days when he painted *The End of the War: Starting Home.* His paintings have become more decorative, and less rugged and virile.

The frame is decorated with carvings made by his own hand and nailed upon it. The forms, the dark oily color and the gritty textures of these bas-reliefs are those of the painted pigment converted into carved wood.

190

PPIN *The End of the War: Starting Home.* 1933. Collection Philadelphia Museum of Art.

191

GEORGE AULONT and *The Arrival of the "New Order" in Crete.*
Now in the Collection of M. Martin Janis, Buffalo.

CHAPTER TWENTY-ONE·

GEORGE AULONT

GEORGE AULONT was born on May 6th, 1888 in Greece, of a comfortable middle-class family. His mother was a native of the Island of Crete, a school teacher, and a descendant of an old island family. She died when he was eight years old. His father was a physician, the son of a clergyman, and a

192

native of the island of Skyros "where," George says, "the celebrated English poet Brooke is buried on a hillside overlooking the waters of the northern Aegean Sea." His father died when he was fourteen, and after his death, George spent two years in Constantinople with an uncle, also a physician. He attended the Evangelical High School of Smyrna.

In Aulont's letter he tells of his later experiences, of his adventures, of his ideas:

I arrived in the U.S.A. in 1907 and as a young lad without training and of an adventurous and carefree nature I travelled a lot, changing jobs and experiencing the usual difficulties of all young people who bite off more than they can chew. But I managed it. I have been a salesman, toy-mechanic, handyman, rough work carpenter, painter. I was in the Army transport service both in the Gulf of Mexico, occupation of Vera Cruz, 1914, and also in the Pacific Coast. Like many of us, I served in the U. S. Army (honorable discharge). I went to Mexico, Tampico on the Panuco River early in 1914 aboard the yacht "Wakiwa" of the late oil king Ed. Doheny, also visited Vera Cruz, Tuxpam, Coazacoalcos (Puerto Mexico on the Isthmus of Tehuantepec). Made a trip to Alaska. So, in a few words, a sort of useless but not dull life.

Many of my friends shook their heads and sanctimoniously pronounced that a rolling stone gathers no moss, but my, what they have missed in life. The Pacific Isles, the Evergreen Mountain ranges in the coast of British Columbia and Alaska. The deserts of New Mexico and Arizona. The most beautiful race of people, the Tehuanas in Mexico. The love of Nature, and the free air you breathe, seeing new people.

I began to paint in 1936. I tried back in 1910 but after a few weeks gave the thing up. Mount Smolika, the 8,000 ft. peak in Epirus, N. W. Greece, was, as you know, the scene of the annihilation of two picked divisions of the Sawdust Caesar's army of the invasion. The magnificent courage and contempt for death of the Greek troops gave me the idea of painting and naming it *On Mount Smolika*.

My hobby is raising canaries, and at this time I have twenty-three, but I have had many more.

I do hope that the day is near so that a new dawn will rise and the people of this accursed planet will come to their senses, disarm, have peace, allot some space to persecuted minorities so that they too can develop their own culture. Then they can fight the forces of nature, floods, droughts, etc., eradicate disease, encourage learning, music, sports, arts, literature. What a world. And what a world is coming.

I must conclude with the Socratean moral *Know Thyself*, live and let live (not however tolerating Fascism, injustice, ignorance, greed or stupidity).

And so, as the Greeks say, Ya-soo (health to you all).

Aulont has never exhibited except in the 1941 Independent show, where his passionately expressed *On Mt. Smolika* stood out as one of the most striking canvases on view.

On Mt. Smolika

INSPIRED BY the courage and bravery of the small Greek army, the artist depicts the advance of his fellow countrymen upon Mt. Smolika in the Autumn of 1940, at the height of Greek victories over invading Italian armies.

The captain who is also the flagbearer leads his men up the steep slopes of the mountain in saw-toothed ascent. The corporal and sergeant also have key positions, one in advance of the lower group of men and the other manning the cannon. The men are dressed in olive drab field uniforms with kilted skirt and cream colored tights strapped at the knee with cording. Their red slippers are bedecked with blue pom-poms and their fezzes with long tassels. Many of the men are blonde with blue eyes, the type which the artist points out is characteristic of this part of the country.

One of the soldiers who has exposed himself to enemy fire has been wounded, but the hazards of war are presented not so much in the soldiers themselves as in the background against which they appear. Although their guns and cannon are not in action, the remarkably painted surface of the mountainside, applied with heavily loaded brush, is slashed upon the canvas, bursting dynamically about the men. These patterns seem to form a resistance to their every step. The light and dark nervous accents of the snow and mud have the abrupt quality and character of drapes on Byzantine Madonnas, and the faces on the men have the look and sharp modeling of those that appear in Greek Orthodox wall paintings.

In the background warclouds hover over the mountain.

AULONT   *On Mt. Smolika.* 1941

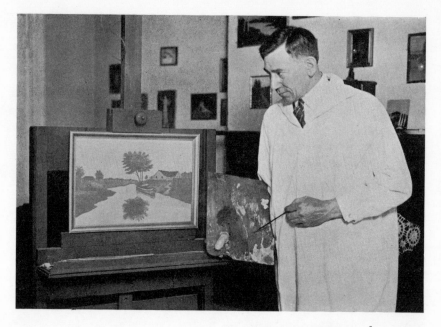

EMILE BRANCHARD, about 1923.

CHAPTER TWENTY-TWO

EMILE BRANCHARD

BONNIE BRANCHARD, wife of the late Emile Branchard, and Stephen Bourgeois, who discovered him, give the following composite picture of him:

Emile Pierre Branchard was born in MacDougal Street in Greenwich Village in 1881. When he was a child his mother moved to 61 Washington Square, which became known as the "House of Genius"—Mme. Branchard's rooming house for artists. He was schooled by French nuns, and he and his mother usually conversed in French.

196

At first he worked at various jobs. For a while he was a truck driver, and during World War I, became a policeman on the Home Defense Force. Exposed to all kinds of weather while searching the waterfront for contraband, he contracted tuberculosis, and his doctor ordered complete quiet. He never read, was bored, and one day began to paint, using the paints, brushes and canvases left behind by one of the artist-roomers who had skipped without paying his bill.

Of his painting, Dorothy C. Miller of the Museum of Modern Art wrote in the catalogue to the *Masters of Popular Painting* exhibition:

His stepfather was a painter who had been a pupil of Meissonier. Emile never had any art training but when he was a boy he used sometimes to watch his stepfather paint and think how he could probably do much better himself.

Mme. Branchard's parlor was filled with her husband's Meissonier-paintings, but when Emile began to paint, his own poetic pictures were kept in the cellar.

Emile was a good cook, and said painting was just like cooking, "you must have the right ingredients and know how to mix them." He said "Colors are like men and women. Some mix and some don't. When they do, it's marriage and when they don't it's divorce." When he felt like painting, he bought a canvas and stretcher and put it on his easel. He then went about with his house chores and each time he passed through the room, he looked at the blank canvas. All at once he saw a picture upon it, and put it down in paint.

A roomer who saw Emile at work in the basement insisted that he send a painting to the Independent show. He was unwilling to do so, and she took two small paintings there herself. Here—it was 1919—Stephen Bourgeois found them and at once gave Branchard a one-man show at his New York gallery, with subsequent showings until 1932. Branchard died in February, 1938, in the house where he had lived for fifty years.

Bonnie Branchard, the artist's fifth wife, gives this additional thumbnail portrait of him: He was good-natured, generous, irresponsible. He was 6'2" tall. He loved to paint trees, snow, and sky, but humans did not interest him; he did not find them beautiful. When asked how he achieved his effects, Branchard said, "Any damn fool can do it—here are the paints and brushes. Surely you have something in your head that wants to be painted, go ahead and paint it."

Branchard was left-handed, and although he painted his pictures with his left hand, he signed them with his right—a result of discipline in school.

Bourgeois once asked him why he did not paint from nature, and he replied: "Because nature runs faster than you can catch her."

Farm in Winter

BRANCHARD'S BLEAK and stark and pure winter is American to the core, the America of Whittier's *Snow-Bound*. The empty corral, the wide deserted landscape, give a sense of vastness, of loneliness. The house squatting like an old dog amongst the protective clumps of thorny trees is a winter oasis. Its color is welcome to the eye very much as the house itself would be to a lonely and half-frozen wayfarer coming up over the hill in the foreground near the artist's signature. For against the dead white snow, its gold yellow sides and brown green roofs are a warming sight.

Spreading as far as the eye can see, the virgin snow lies over the earth. If the snow had fallen fresh it would spot the trees and cover the rooftops, but it does not, and seems to have been on the ground for a long time. Not a living thing has been this way since it fell, for there are no traces or paths in the snow. The cloudless pastel sky carries the loneliness to the farthest reaches of the heavens.

RANCHARD *Farm in Winter.* Collection Marie Harriman.

JOSEPHINE JOY working on *Mission Valley Farm.*

200

CHAPTER TWENTY-THREE

JOSEPHINE JOY

A quaint village called North River Mills, Hampshire County, West Virginia, was the place of my birth. The date was September 1, 1869. My parents, of English and Scotch ancestry, had nine children, three boys and six girls, I being the youngest. My father moved his family to Illinois and we lived on a farm near Pekin for a while, later moving to Pekin where I acquired my education and religious training.

At an early age my ability to sketch was apparent by the work I did, sketching birds, trees and flowers. This gift coming to the attention of relatives, then teachers and friends, I was advised to develop that talent. Circumstances, however, prevented me from following my tendency in that direction until later on in life.

When through necessity I felt led by Divine guidance to pursue that which I laid aside in my youth and had faith that I could paint pictures if given an opportunity, it was a struggle at first but, I soon found that I could blend and harmonize the various shades of oils. I love to paint in the open sitting in some beautiful garden, hillside or remote place or in Balboa Park where I have sketched many pictures.

My idea in my mind is to find a subject that appeals to me, then I outline all objects in detail. I might add a few blossoms, butterflies or whatever fits into the picture, keeping in mind at all times whatever I am painting as a whole. I paint from nature but occasionally find myself designing. I like to paint landscapes, but flowers and gardens, still life interest me too. I paint because I love the work, it gives me something tangible to look forward to. I feel that I am doing something that is worthwhile, that others will enjoy now and in after years.

I was married at the age of eighteen to Francis Bradley, of this union two children were born, a daughter and a son both living. Mr. Bradley passed away. Later I was given a position as saleslady in the Fur Department at Marshall Fields in Chicago, later I was promoted to decorator in the same department, was in their employ for several years, during which time I married Mr. Joy. His health failing we moved to California in 1924, and he passed away in California in 1927. Since then I have had reverses and financial losses. I sold my home and I am now painting pictures.

Josephine Joy was on the California Art Project in Los Angeles from 1936 to 1939, and during this time she painted over 100 canvases. Elliott Torrey, San Diego artist, recognized the merit of her work on the project, and interested others. It was called to my attention in the east by Roland J. McKinney and Reginald Poland. In 1940 her paintings were publicly exhibited for the first time and the same year the canvas *My Gift to You* won a $25 prize at the

26th Annual Art Guild Exhibit held at the San Diego Museum of Fine Arts. A group of her paintings has been shown at the California Art Project in Los Angeles and her pictures have been included in group shows at both the Los Angeles Museum of Fine Art and the Stendahl Galleries.

Dream Garden

THE PAINTING, *Dream Garden* by Josephine Joy is a flower garden of her memories, a composite of many gardens which she has known. Her flowers, trees and vines, which she knows intimately and loves wholeheartedly, are brought together here and arranged into a vari-colored and fanciful bouquet.

The garden path in neutral buff tones serves as an eye rest against the galaxy of color in the flora. It is shaped like a strange marine animal whose tentacles reach out and hold together the separate garden memories.

In a later version of this painting, the vine which appears below the watering can reminded the artist so persistently of a snake that she actually painted in a serpent's head. This confirms the impression one gets that *Dream Garden* is really a Garden of Eden picture, a fantasy of flora and fauna, and it is quite conceivable that in a still later version of the painting, Adam and Eve may appear along one of the paths.

202

y *Dream Garden.* 1936.   Collection WPA Southern California Art Project, Los Angeles.

SAMUEL KOCH at work on *Coney Island*.

CHAPTER TWENTY-FOUR

SAMUEL KOCH

SAMUEL KOCH has written the following autobiography:

I was born Samuel Kochmeister on November 13th, 1887, in Warsaw, Poland. When I reached the age of six, my family moved to a small village. As there were no schools there, the only schooling I had was what my father, after a hard day's work, could give me. This was mostly of a religious nature. At the age of fourteen I left home to earn my own livelihood. Working all day, I did not have any time to go to school, so I read in my spare time.

At the age of 19, I started traveling, and in 1910 came to New York. After spending about three years there, and working at various trades, I again got the urge to wander, working among other places, at Ford, National Biscuit and on the docks. After 2 years I returned to New York to be among my friends.

204

They got me interested in a dramatic club, where I became very active. In this same club, I met the girl who later became my wife. We have just celebrated our twenty-fifth anniversary and have two lovely children, a son and a daughter.

One day when my son was three years old, he asked me to make a picture for him. He had brought over a book of Shakespeare's works which had his picture there. I sat down with pencil and paper and copied the picture. The likeness was so remarkable that I, myself, was really astonished. From then on, I began to copy everything I saw.

Not being able to earn a living, we bought a candy store. As little leisure as I had then, I still found time to do my drawing. I remarked to my wife, half in jest, that some day I would be an artist. She told me that only when I started doing original work would she consider me an artist. At this time a friend of mine who owned a water color set which he never used, made a present of it to me. I then started experimenting with colors, and made my first original painting. Soon after that, my wife had to undergo a major operation and we had to give up the store almost for nothing. After she returned from the hospital, I went to work in the millinery line. As the seasons in this line are very short, I had much more time to paint, but I had very little money to buy painting materials.

I had a great urge to paint, but at times I became very discouraged. At these times, my family proved to be a great help to me. I remember one time on my birthday I came home to find an easel and paints, which my family had bought for me.

The first time my work was shown publicly was in 1938 when an oil of mine was exhibited in the yearly show for new men at the A.C.A. Gallery. The following Fall three of my works were invited by Miss Francis, director of the Contemporary Art Galleries, and to my surprise all three were accepted by the jury. Mr. Janis at this time became interested in my work and visited my home to see the rest of my paintings. He selected three pictures for the exhibition of *Unknown American Painters*. It was at this time that my first painting was sold, *The Flood*. Since then several of my paintings were in exhibitions, and encouraged, I made many very large oils. Other exhibitions followed where single examples of my work were shown and eventually an art dealer, Mr. Charell, saw a recent painting at the Contemporary Art and in 1941 took sixteen of my paintings to Hollywood, where ten of them were included in a showing with examples of well-known artists.

Through all the years that I visited exhibitions and tried to develop myself and my art, I never once let myself be influenced by other artists, but always tried to go my own way. How far I succeeded I will let others judge.

I do not make a problem of color. I stick my brush in the paint and go ahead and paint, and put on the color. I believe that art is just a part of the whole cultural life such as books, theatre including drama, opera and movies. When a man writes a story I believe he means me or some of my friends. So the motive of artists of all kinds is to show the people their own life like a mirror and I believe the painter has the same purpose to reflect the life of the people. That is why I paint things the way I see them.

Being one of the masses, I try to paint in our common language, without any puzzles. I want to be understood. I like to paint in bright colors because there is plenty of

205

misery and darkness in the world, and I think a painting should be something that should bring happiness and joy. Naturally, I, as everyone else, have my dark moments, as some of my paintings show, but I try not to dwell on them too long, and I always return to the brighter side of life in my paintings.

Union Square

THROUGH THE very center of the painting, Koch has cut his composition vertically and horizontally, as well as obliquely in both directions. At the hub of these radiating lines, stands a group of people assembled alongside a monument.

The obliques form a central motive which is shaped like an hourglass; the buildings are the upper half, and at the neck the people pass through vertically, pouring out upon the broadening walk—the lower part of the hourglass, in the foreground—where they assume various casual positions and natural attitudes. Koch has given character and meaning to these figures by an intimate and sympathetic understanding of their habits of thought and action.

In color, the light grey walks, shaded by darker greys, and the mottled cool greens of nature, are the two dominant notes. Darker tones in the figures and the multi-colored buildings make pleasing color alternates.

Omission of many shadows where ordinarily encountered, and the unexpected introduction of others from opposite directions, come as a surprise.

206

Union Square. 1936   Collection Ludwig Charell.

207

FLORA LEWIS and *Christ and the Woman at the Well.*

CHAPTER TWENTY-FIVE

FLORA LEWIS

FLORA CARNELL LEWIS was born Jan. 12, 1903, in Atchison, Kansas. Of her life Mrs. Lewis writes:

Started painting and drawing as a small child about the age of six years, watching my father draw a mule which I thought I could draw better than he. I certainly enjoyed drawing and the best of all drawing pictures of my teachers. Of all the Art

I have done I have never studied it in School; But I love it. I am a lover of Art, Not only with pencil and Brush; But Needlework, Crotcheting, Knitting, Music, Embroidery and Sewing.

. . . After ten years of employment as a maid at the Atchison Hospital I retired and was married to Dr. Percy Lewis, Veterinary of Marshall Mo., in 1938. I devoted most of my time as House Wife, Seamstress, and used my painting only as a retreat.

. . . I painted the *Interpretation of Sin Surrounding the Churches*, for a Union Revival Service in which the two pastors were conducting. This picture consisted of the Serpent's (representative of Sin) Body and tail wrapped around the two churches.

. . . upon which the Pastors Based their Sermonettes. They had 32 converts and Rev. Fitch uses this painting for Revival services in Various Towns and States. He had 22 converts in Dalton, Mo.

. . . My husband was an appreciator of Art and Lover of animals. Being a Veterinary in which his interest lay and a Farm Boy, at his request I painted *Farm Life*. Dr. Lewis of evenings when he came home would tell me of the good times he had in his boyhood days, driving his Gray horse and buggy taking his friends to church And his boyhood days on the Farm an Old Homestead.

Aug. 16, 1940 Dr. Lewis lost his life, instantly hit by a coal truck. This happening has become a Great Sorrow and sadness in my life which it seems impossible to forget.

Farm Life

DESCRIBING THE painting *Farm Life*, Flora Lewis writes:

I sketched my chickens and geese and turkeys from neighbors' farms. Here's a reasonable joke about one of the turkeys as they say the Turkey is as large as the cow in the water. Answer: Since my Husband was a Veterinary I had him to caponize the turkey (as large as the cow in the water) before I painted him.

The dog and the cat were given to me for a wedding present. The well is a well at my Old Home place in Atchison, Kansas. The woods the hunter and his dogs represent hunting life on the farm.

As you know a home is not complete without children. The children drinking at the well have come home from Sunday School, tired and thirsty for a drink. The flowers around the house add beauty to the picture. The little boy has changed his clothes and put on his overall and the little girl like all girls stays dressed up in her pretty ruffled dress.

The Ducks prove that the Setter Dog is a Bird dog ready to attack the birds on the stream of water. The Rabbit makes up Hunting life on the farm. The water lillies a beautiful Flower on God's Green earth, you find in Various streams of water also the cat tails. The pine trees were on Dr. Lewis' Old HomeStead.

We learn from her letter that *Farm Life* is made up of experiences and impressions gathered from a variety of sources. Some were from her present environment, but others were out of memories, her own and especially her husband's. These separate happenings relate to her central theme, farm life. As isolated groupings they are brought to the picture and assembled there, and the picture retains the flavor of this episodic treatment. However, all the units revolve around the farm house which is set in the heart of the encircling movement, and by this means Flora Lewis integrates her separate elements into a well-organized unit.

I entered *Farm Life* at Dr. Lewis' request and am proud to say I were winner of First prize at Sedalia, Missouri State Fair August 18, 1939, which caused a furor and controversy. Judged by Austin Faricy, Teacher at Stephen State College, Columbia. I am proud of being recognized as an untrained Artist, and proud to be recognized as a member of the Unknown American Painters show, the only Negro woman and the only representative of the State of Missouri.

Controversy pursued this picture. At the time it was being shown at the Museum of Modern Art, the following editorial appeared in *The Art Digest* of November, 1939:

When Is Art Art? The inherent fallacy of the prize system was highlighted this year at the Missouri State Fair, when a Negro housewife, Mrs. Percy Lewis, won the first prize in painting with a conglomerated view of *Farm Life*, as seen from atop a nearby windmill by a bird with cataracts. Flaunting its blue ribbon (and $35) before the canvases of 100 carefully trained artists was this sincerely-scrambled mixture of farm fowl, animals and humans, all crudely delineated on muslin, sans perspective, in oil paint and glittering aluminum shellac.

"It is the finest example of primitive art I have ever seen," commented Austin Faricy, teacher of aesthetics at Stephens College for Women, who judged the contest.

After studying carefully a reproduction in the Kansas City *Star* (not the original muslin), I fear that the chief casualty in this comedy of snobbery is the good Missouri housewife. Aesthetes, bored with it all, have a tendency to sport their superiority by championing unschooled artists. How can Mrs. Lewis be expected to return contentedly to her happy kitchen chores to await a summons from the Modern Museum after such a victory over formal art training?

. . . There have been true primitives in the past—a Joseph Pickett is now valued in the thousands and John Kanes are avidly sought. But, as a rule, only children and highly trained artists can paint a picture so badly that it is good.

210

LEWIS *Farm Life.* 1938

211

So that the readers of a widely circulated art magazine might not fall victim to a common misapprehension, the author answered, and his answer, published in the *Art Digest's* next issue, is repeated here:

Sir: In your editorial "When Is Art Art?" in the Oct. 15th issue of *The Art Digest*, I was interested in your observations on the painting *Farm Life* by Flora Lewis.

It is unfortunate that you did not see the original which was in New York for more than three weeks before your column appeared, but based your appraisal upon a newspaper color-reproduction. In this instance the color-work was so flagrantly off, that, for one example, a soft gray was reproduced as a sharp blue. Since Mrs. Lewis' use of color is vital to the imaginative quality of the picture, distortion in the reproduction makes it difficult to get an integrated idea of the real character of the work.

The picture is not a "conglomerated view" but a well-ordered representation of Flora Lewis' idea of heaven-on-earth. It is a fantasy of abundance, expressed in the farmyard filled with mated fowl and cattle, the plowed earth, the cheerfully-lighted homestead, smoking chimney, lavishly flowing brook, the huntsman and his dog, and finally, the portrait of herself and husband in a horse and buggy. (Fulfillment in her heaven excludes the automobile—her husband is a veterinary.)

Nor is the picture "as seen from atop a nearby windmill." The use of perspective may be unorthodox, but it is logical. Land is of paramount significance to her, and she emphasizes this fact by tilting the landscape toward the observer, as Cezanne would tilt a table-top.

You ask: "How can Mrs. Lewis be expected to return contentedly to her happy kitchen chores to await a summons from the Modern Museum?" The Museum of Modern Art answered your doubt before it was expressed, since this painting had been chosen early in September for inclusion in the Advisory Committee's exhibition *Unknown American Painters*.

The idea underlying this exhibition is to create interest in the work of unknowns, among whom may be artists of distinction in forms of expression whose merits we do not properly evaluate. Perhaps among them may be artists equal to Pickett or Kane, who you concede were "true primitives in the past." The need for this work is so apparent that to prove the point one need go no further than your book *Modern American Painting* published October 3, which still does not include one of these two "true primitives," namely Pickett. I ask the time-worn question: if such artists exist unknown today, must they be dead before their work is known and understood?

212

CHAPTER TWENTY-SIX

JESSIE PREDMORE

WHEN JESSIE PREDMORE was two years old, her father took up a homestead among the Indians on the Nez Percés reservation in Idaho. Her playmates were Indian children. Of this period she writes:

There was no water on the Indian reserve, so they used the springs that were on our place and for the use of the water, we had the use of their horses. We rode six miles to school on horseback. I would try to ride any horse that was on the place, and if I couldn't find a horse lively enough for me, I would try a cow.

Our first few years on the homestead were hard sledding. Next to the oldest child in a family of ten, I had been born in Osco, Ill., Jan. 30th, 1896 of French-Canadian parents. My older brother was never very strong and so hard work was my lot.

213

The Indian women showed mother how to make moccasins so we didn't have shoes until we started school, then we changed as soon as we got home. Mother was eighteen years older than I, so we grew up together, you might say.

As a child, luxuries were few at our place, so to have paints couldn't even be thought of. We used to take the different colored clays that we could find around the place and it was just too bad if my father had any linseed oil. If not, goodbye to the salad oil. If neither was available, the next best thing was water.

The Indians interested me a great deal and I intend to devote a great deal of my pictures to the life of the Indians.

When Jessie was twelve, her folks moved to a ranch

around which the canyon made a complete circle. Then we had no neighbors at all. I went in nurse's training at 14, and got married at 16, starting right out to cook for a crew of men. We came to California in 1917, during the last war, and I started nursing again. I have always worked to help raise a family of three children.

My marriage broke up in 1932 and I was dejected for four years. During this time, I took to sketching. I have now married again, and my husband is with me 100% in my work. I paint whenever I can find the time.

I began painting in oils in January, 1940, and have twelve pictures now. Six pictures were shown at the Hagen Art Galleries at Stockton and seven at Sacramento, the Crocker Art Galleries. In my pictures, I believe I have a story to tell. As to the choice of color, I use the color that suits me best. I have the picture thoroughly in my mind before I start painting, to each and every detail. I am very pleased with my work and only hope other people can see in it just what I intend the picture to convey.

The author is indebted to Dr. Grace L. McCann Morley, director of the San Francisco Museum, who called this artist to his attention.

She's Gone

ONE DOES not have to be a professional detective to be able to construct the story behind this picture. It is full of evidence bearing on the emotional theme—anger and remorse.

The emptied drawer, clothes hangers flung upon the closet floor, an empty picture frame thrown on the dresser, and the tell-tale note dropped on the floor, all point to the vexed and hurried departure of the young wife.

It is 3 a.m. The forlorn young man with the rumpled hair, sitting with his head in his hands, has been through a sleepless night. The disheveled bed, the half-smoked cigarettes on the side-table, reflect his distraught state,

214

but through all of this, one pillow remains untouched. Graphically under-scoring his unsettled condition and mental anguish is the off-square arrange-ment of bed and dresser and the tilting floor, an unusually sophisticated composition for a self-taught artist.

Colors are smoky and give to the painting a dull cast as if the interior were dimly lighted in the dead of night, thus augmenting the doleful feeling.

But let us examine the scene further to see if things are really as bad as they seem. The pillow cases are bordered with tiny red spotted embroidery and the careful needle work of the crisp new doilies, matched on the night table and dresser, though simple, give every evidence that this is trousseau linen. So it may be but a temperamental quarrel—an early marital tiff. We are suddenly aware that this is more than a probability when we notice the dog has pricked up his ears and turned his head expectantly, as if he senses returning footsteps.

215

The man who put
Historical Poems
in the
Grand Opera
and
Nobel Prize
Contests.

MARITIME CO., Fenway, Boston, Massachusetts.

THE POET KING

Bids received for rights to 8 Plays, 150 G. E. Lothrop Poems, 40 Songs and and Photo rights of the "Poet King". Also for interest in new Moving Picture invention, revolutionizing the business, improving the films 200 pr. ct., and making $2.00 picture houses a success.

MARITIME CO.
Fenway,   Boston,   Massachusetts

GEORGE E. LOTHROP, Reverse side of the painting, *The Revelers!*

216

CHAPTER TWENTY-SEVEN

GEORGE E. LOTHROP

AFTER MONTHS of searching, the mystery surrounding the life and death of Lothrop remains as baffling as ever. It was Peter Hunt of Provincetown who found a group of his paintings in a Boston junk store not long ago. If it were not for this, we might not even have known that Lothrop existed. Hunt's enthusiasm for the paintings was contagious and now many of his friends share his pleasure.

At his suggestion, I visited Helena Rubinstein at Greenwich, Conn., where I saw *The Revelers!,* an exciting dish of pigment. The only concrete evidence remaining to give some direct information about the artist is in the form of two stickers which were found pasted to the back panel of this painting, but they tell a good deal about his activities and colorful personality. Most of the text on these stickers is legible in the reproduction on the opposite page. The text in his own hand under the picture *The Poet King,* reads:

THE POET KING

Copyrighted 1912 by Geo. E. Lothrop, Boston,

Plays, Songs, Monologues, Poems, Novels, etc.

According to his own record, he envisioned himself as *The Poet King* surrounded by bathing beauties of yesteryear. This is a photograph of himself in a fantastic costume as Father Neptune, and the bathing girls are cutouts pasted around him. According to this advertisement, he wrote eight plays, 150 poems, and forty songs, and invented a motion picture device "revolutionizing the business, improving the films 200 pr. ct., and making $2.00 picture houses a success", aside from putting "Historical Poems in the Grand Opera and Nobel Prize Contests."

The Maritime Co., Fenway, Boston, Mass., was evidently the commercial guise under which he himself offered his diverse talents to the world. In this technique of presentation, as well as in his many-faceted creative activities, he is reminiscent of our already legendary Louis Eilshemius, of whom he was a contemporary.

Fortunately Lothrop dated some of his paintings, and we know that he was still working in 1929, the latest date recorded on his work. This late work was a landscape in a strange variation of pointillist technique in which the dots of many bright colors obviously suggested numberless tiny visages and heads which he painted into the mountainside, trees and heavens.

The Revelers!

THE REVELERS! is truly a bacchanale, ecstatic, abandoned, obsessed. The temple setting and the lavish theatrical-Egyptian costumes suggest "Aida" as inspiration: Lothrop was fond of the opera. The mass of wild-eyed dancing girls descending the steps directly toward the observer, their hair streaming, their arms flailing the air in loosely coordinated gestures, make a picture of mad gaiety.

Below in the lagoon are dozens of male human heads bobbing about, interspersed by the heads of other creatures fabulously conceived and concealed in the waves.

Just as a bank of clouds, a strangely shaped tree, the profile of a hill, sometimes bring to mind an unrelated image, so here the artist found in the configuration of his brush strokes and in the contours and colors of the choppy water, suggestions for these quasi-human and animal heads. In this respect, the picture, painted more than twenty years ago, utilizes what is today called the *paranoiac image* in painting, random shapes suggesting concrete objects which are developed and incorporated into the composition.

Wild as the tempo may be, it is stepped up in the background, where flying nudes and wide bands of vivid color—red, white, blue and gold—streak across the sky.

The many Ensor-like faces and masks are arbitrarily scaled, that is, they vary in size irrespective of their true relation to each other or distance from the observer. The largest of all appears in the very background; emerging out of the streaked skies, it is like the man-in-the-moon turned harlequin for the occasion.

218

LOTHROP   *The Revelers!*   Collection Mme. Helena Rubinstein.

CHAPTER TWENTY-EIGHT

CHARLES M. JOHNSON

JOHNSON HAS written the following about his work:

In my youth I was greatly enrapt with the art of wood-engraving as a beautiful medium, as it was used in the three leading magazines, Harper's, Scribner's and the Century. In this field there was sufficient remuneration for sustenance, which I meant to use as a stepping stone for higher art studies, but unfortunately when I was ready to enter the field it began to decline so rapidly that my opportunity was hopelessly lost.

Then came in the process of photo-engraving, chemically and mechanically produced in mass production and of course much cheaper, and publishers took advantage of this. Of necessity I had to switch to this field for a livelihood. But in all these intervening years, I made numerous outdoor sketches in landscapes, and I was greatly enchanted with the fleeting atmospheric beauty of nature, using as a landscape painter must, the three dimensions, both linear and aerial perspective, and if it is so rendered that the fourth dimension can be felt or perceived, then all the finer. But the fourth dimension lies largely with the feeling or conception of the spectator.

Johnson, born in Sweden in 1862, came to America in 1881. He had some lessons in drawing at Cooper Union, New York, in 1896. It was thirty years later, however, that he began to paint.

In 1920 he first exhibited at the Society of Independent Artists, and has since sent pictures there at various intervals. The 1941 exhibit included an interesting portrait of *Roosevelt Speaking, 1932.* This portrait appears in the photograph above.

Oslo Winter

JOHNSON's *Oslo Winter Scene* is so frigid that the snow is literally blue with cold. Deeply tinted, it is "just as it looks on cold days," he avers. The sky is dark, almost gun metal grey, and this heavy color against the snow-covered scene adds greatly to the feeling of long-entrenched winter in the North Country. But the houses in tones of tan grey, biscuit tans, yellow and peach offer warmth to the scene, and in defiance of the laws of perspective, the windows both on the front and sides of the houses frankly and squarely face the observer even though the street itself recedes into deep space. This together with the warm tone of the houses imparts the feeling of welcome. One exception, however, is to be noted. On a two-tone house, the upper windows recede in perspective, and fittingly enough, the facade here is cool in color. Below, where the tone is warmer, the window again faces forward.

The horse and sled coming directly toward us are so drawn as to seem a single object, and its isolation is enhanced by reason of the fact that nothing else animate is in sight.

Upon the hill behind the houses grow evergreens, and the slope is strikingly patterned by snow against rock, forming an arresting contrast with the other areas, which are flat.

The paint is applied in almost purist technique. Each house is given its own surface textures as are the rooftops and sky, and the large shape of the foreground snow is smooth, broken only by faint slightly bluer tracks denoting sparse traffic.

222

JHNSON *Oslo Winter.* 1933

223

PA HUNT   1934. "The borrowed palette is only a pose."

CHAPTER TWENTY-NINE

PA HUNT

PA HUNT, horseman, sportsman, born in New York in 1870, lost his fortune in 1920, just nine years before this became fashionable. He left his Christian name behind with his old life and moved to Provincetown where, as Pa, he lived with his wife and son Peter until the end of his days. He had his garden and his dog Jimmy and loved to spin great yarns, for which he won a considerable reputation.

Living in this community of artists over a period of years whetted his curiosity about painting. He felt he could do as well as a great many of the well-known artists who came to Provincetown, and by way of a first achievement did what his son calls a "neat bit of utilitarian decoration" for his kitchen. The Hunts had many guests during the hot summer days, and over the sink, where it would be clearly visible, Pa painted a mural, a frigid winter scene, air-conditioning both guests and himself by visual suggestion.

224

T *Way Up Along: Provincetown.* Collection Peter Hunt, Provincetown.

225

Then he found an old frame in the cellar, covered it with a piece of bed-sheet and made his first easel picture. It was a whaling scene and he submitted it to the jury for the Provincetown annual exhibition in 1931. He was pleasantly surprised when it was accepted, and even more so when it created considerable comment. With this encouragement he continued to paint, devoting his long winters to it, but only the winters, since his summers were reserved for other pursuits.

His first one-man exhibition was held in the Morton Galleries, New York, a few months after he died in 1934. In 1938 two canvases were included in the *Popular Masters* show, and a second one-man show was arranged in 1939 at the Grace Horne Galleries, Boston.

Pa Hunt had a unique way of working. He squeezed his colors directly onto his brush, mixing them on the canvas. He claimed that "using a palette was wasteful in paint, energy, and time." Pa always took his achievements casually and half-believed that those who admired his work were "jollying him along."

Way Up Along: Provincetown

THIS INTIMATE street scene is Pa Hunt's Provincetown. It is like a garden of houses fenced in by the sidewalks. One notices first the tremendous tree with its branchy structure and next to it the street that never ends, that once started, goes on and up and out of the top of the picture frame. The dog on the sidewalk trails a curious individual—a man with a transparent torso through which we see the fence uninterruptedly. Special properties also belong to the tree, for although we feel its huge volume of foliage, actually the mass of leaves lies in back of its structure, which is completely in view.

The picture's technique gives it an iridescent diffusion and it is expressionist in its free, bold line. It is altogether a combination of these two qualities, sensitive and poetic seeing and decisive statement. Its direct emotional release has not prevented Hunt from obtaining an interestingly coordinated composition made up of large, general space divisions and diminutive and detailed space segments.

226

WILLIAM S. MULHOLLAND in Rupert, Vt., 1934

CHAPTER THIRTY

WILLIAM S. MULHOLLAND

WILLIAM SHERMAN MULHOLLAND was born March 13, 1870, in Wither-bee, N. Y. He studied for the ministry at the Troy Conference Academy, Poultney, Vt., and Syracuse University and was eventually ordained a minister in the Methodist Church. He married a schoolmate, and they had a family of four daughters and two sons, all of whom were sent to college in spite of the modest earnings of one in his calling.

One of his daughters, Mrs. Helen M. Ranney, has written of her father:

I think many have thought it strange that one with father's love of beauty and ability to create did not discover this earlier in life. My explanation is this: Father was a man of great physical force. He enjoyed and needed using his strength. Until his strength declined, the hours spent in the necessary study to prepare his sermons were as much as his body could bear to be confined. Favorite vents for his strength were vegetable and flower gardens, chickens, wood pile, house-plants, horse to care for, much driving and walking too.

Many will remember father for his great sense of humor. He also had the ability to put people at ease. He had a way of adjusting himself to people and surroundings so that very humble people did not feel condescended to. Father's great size, 6'3", made his usual gentlemanly manner seem incongruous.

. . . I think he painted quite rapidly. When an idea possessed him, he gave it all he had until he was weary, often too weary. After he had ruined many shirts and trousers, I made him a voluminous apple-green smock which he wore and used for a cleaning cloth for his hands. He rigged an old washstand for an easel which he used for several years. Then mother gave him a real easel. . . .

I have been surprised that the colors purple and lavender did not appear more often in father's paintings. He was extremely fond of these colors.

In *Mt. Antoine*, owned by Mrs. Elizabeth Hine of Albany, Mulholland obtained a vibrant purple by juxtaposing red and blue. Obviously he did not know about Pointillism. Still by placing spots of blue next to spots of red, he gained atmospheric purples on his distant mountain sides. When Mrs. Hine acquired this painting in 1934, the artist remarked that he had found it difficult to mix the color that would give the proper effect, and after experimenting, hit upon this way of getting it "just as he wanted it."

His daughter's letter continues:

Father called his most sincere critic a little boy who was 8 or 9 years old and who often called to watch father paint. Father always got out what he was working on (he usually had several going at a time) and asked the boy for his opinions. He told father just what he thought of them. . . .

I doubt if any of the courses at school gave him any adequate help in finding an outlet for the aesthetic side of his nature which I believe was strong in him. I remember as a small child, his attempt to learn to play the piano. It seemed to go too slowly and anyhow, his fingers were so large that it was hard to strike only one key at a time. He also attempted writing, but never got beyond a few pages. His poetic phase immediately preceded his discovery that he could paint.

I don't think he ever sketched any of his pictures before painting them. The picture began with the actual painting. He had a great mind for detail. I think his memory for scenes might almost be called photographic.

William Mulholland was a yearly exhibitor at the Manchester show after 1932. Several of his canvases found purchasers, mostly among the artists. In September, 1935, he wrote to the artist Henry Schakenberg:

. . . to sincerely thank you and to say to you that it means a great deal to me to have one of your exceptional ability as an artist purchase a canvas of mine. . . . I find a great deal of personal satisfaction in the work as a kind of side issue or hobby.

A one-man show of 70 examples of his work was held in Rupert, Vt., in 1935. His canvas, *Maple Sugar Making in Vermont*, acquired by Harriette Miller, in 1934, and reproduced here, was included in the show of *Unknowns* in 1939.

The Rev. Mulholland had begun painting by doing church posters, which were usually very bright, with every letter a different color. For a Christmas gift in 1925 he received a $1 set of paints from his wife, and it was this gift that started him on his painting career. She was very proud of his accomplishments and he in turn was more pleased for her than he was for himself.

After the sudden death of his wife a few months before his own, he wrote to Mrs. Endress, a former teacher and life-long friend:

I have known "our dear girl" as you lovingly refer to her in your letter, for about 45 years, very intimately and I have not known a purer sweeter more patient and sacrificing spirit than was she. A most devoted wife and so patient with my topsy turvy temperament through all the years. No family of children were ever more fortunate in a mother than was ours. She lived for us all in the superlative degree.

In mid-August of 1936, Mr. Mulholland brought his paintings to Manchester as usual for the annual exhibition there. Several days later, at the age of 66, he met his death suddenly when a rifle he was about to clean was accidentally discharged.

Maple Sugar Making in Vermont

In *Maple Sugar Making in Vermont*, the Rev. Mulholland achieves color effects not by the actual use of color as such, but in a less obvious way, by juxtaposing almost neutral lights and darks in a way to create color sensation. Never high in key, they still give the impact of strong color intensity.

229

It is not necessary to know that the artist was a minister to see in this picture a strongly religious love of nature. There is an upward surge of the trees whose tiny filigreed branches vibrate to the heavens in spiritual ecstasy, singing halleluiah.

In the foreground the snow is spotted with dark areas. Further on where dark areas predominate, they are in turn spotted with white puffs of snow and steam. This is a transition in which positive and negative forms reverse their relative positions as they move over the canvas. The interchanging of light and dark takes place not only upon the ground but throughout the canvas, and the unexpected reversal of accents makes the picture pulsate.

Mr. Mulholland has been careful to paint a shadow for every tree. He has given to each of the three crows its faithful shadow and to the dog another. But when he painted the horses in the path, he gave the shadow a concrete form. Instead of painting a shadow for the team, he gave the sorrel horse a dark partner in its place. The painter has religiously paired his animals and birds, each with its own shadow for a mate.

The driver of the team is the subject of pictorial wit. The tree on the right of the path is adorned with three pails alongside of each other. The tree directly across the path also has three, but the center pail is replaced this time by the head of the man who drives the sleigh, as if the artist were humorously commenting that the man's mind is on maple sugar.

The composition is not unorthodox but the scale of the figures may seem so. The team and the driver, for example, although in the middle ground, are larger in scale than the figure at the woodpile, ostensibly in the foreground. The three birds on the same picture plane as the diminutive figure are of considerably larger scale.

This is probably due to the fact that Mulholland follows no formal procedure of recessional space, but measures his figures to his own pictorial needs. For instance, if the signature on the canvas represents the spot where the artist stood, the birds logically become the nearest objects, the dog next, and then the man with the team of horses. The man at the shed is set at the bottom of a declivity further removed than the other figures, hence he appears smaller. The entire shed detail is introduced like an insert on an old map—it has its own enclosure and its general scale is slightly altered, orienting it to its allotted space.

230

ULHOLLAND *Maple Sugar Making in Vermont,* 1934. Collection Mr. & Mrs. Harlan Miller, Arlington, Vt.

231

CLEO CRAWFORD and his wife, 1936

CHAPTER THIRTY-ONE

CLEO CRAWFORD

WHILE VISITING the Walter Fleischers at their herb farm in New City one summer's day, I asked if there were any self-taught painters in the vicinity. My question, habitually asked, was now especially prompted by the fact that this was a community where professional painters gather. In such an environment, there generally are non-professionals who are attracted by the activity of artists to the point where they begin to paint, usually because social approval enables them to leap this first hurdle.

My host replied that he had heard of one. I was delighted at the prospect of a possible adventure, and we set out to find the man and see his work.

Entering Haverstraw, we crossed to the "wrong side of the tracks," where

232

there stood a row of unpainted, weatherbeaten shacks, all very much alike but one. This house was set apart by the fact that nailed to the verandah post for all the world to see, was an oil painting, very bright in color, very primitive in execution. No sign, no additional information was necessary. Here was a touching story. Here were poverty, obscurity, and the creative impulse.

Mrs. Crawford, who met us at the door, invited us in, and upon entering we beheld several other striking canvases which dominated the dreary walls. We became suddenly aware that the painter lay ill upon a cotbed, in a corner near the only window of what proved to be the living-dining-bedroom.

Cleo Crawford, 47, Negro laborer, painter in his spare time, was so pleased to have unexpected visitors, that he sat up and smiled, apologized for being ill, put on a robe, and entered eagerly into the conversation.

After a short stay, we each selected and purchased a painting, *Telegraph Pole* and *Christmas*. As a memento, I cherish a scrap of paper on which is a joint receipt for the two pictures.

Our visit had caused considerable curiosity amongst the small Negro children in the neighborhood, who kept peeping in at the doorway, and as we left with the paintings, they joined us in a procession across the road. Immediately after, neighbors descended upon the Crawfords to hear the news.

A month later, I visited Crawford's home again, and was shocked to learn he was in the hospital. He was never to recover from his illness. After undergoing a series of operations, he succumbed before the year was out. In the fall before he died, he was to receive his first public recognition. His painting *Christmas* was included in the group showing of *Unknowns*. Naturally the economic factor was of first importance to Crawford. Still he was an artist and it was a comfort to him to receive this recognition "by a museum."

Christmas

PAINTED ON the reverse side of oilcloth, framed by the artist with pieces of brass curtain rod attached by brass tacks, *Christmas* is Crawford's portrayal of the spirit of the season. Flowers are in bloom. Chicks wander on the lawn,

233

animals gambol and the birds on the trees lend gaiety to the occasion. Colors too are in spirit; bright reds, blues and mahoganies which trim the white house as if freshly painted by the owner, are placed in a setting of verdant trees. The flowered curtains are in place with wreaths decorating every window. The well next to the house, topped by a cross upon which stands a "dove," becomes a sort of religious symbol of the occasion—Christmas in the deep South.

The two-dimensional quality in the picture is a predominant characteristic. Only the front elevation of the objects is seen. No roof or sides appears on the house or well, nor have the water pails any volume. The steps on which the woman stands are flattened like a rug. The rows of flat color areas of slate grey, green and purples at the bottom, which designate the ground in front of the house, add nothing to the depth of space, but on the contrary act as a foundation of color layers upon which stand the house, trees, water well, pail, as well as both figures. Crawford has elementally placed all of them on the horizon line.

As a part of this elemental concept, the lowest branch of the tree on the right follows the slant of the roof but the leaves do not overlap it. Similarly, on the opposite side of the house a branch narrowly escapes collision with the chimney.

Vigorous painting passages are found in the contrasts that exist between the tense leaves of the trees and the white clouds and heliotrope skies which pierce through. Because everything remains on the same picture plane, the purple blues amid the greens become tropical flowers on the trees. The vibrant counterpattern caused by the leaves and spreading branches against the skies relieves the static horizontals and verticals of the architecture.

An amusing touch and incidentally the only direct representation of depth is found in the cat which is seen within and without the window frame at one and the same time. Standing on the sill between the curtains, it is possessed of an immateriality which allows its tail to pass through the window pane and into the open.

Controlled as the picture is in its division of spaces, it is still fresh and spontaneous in spirit, and the very crudeness with which it is painted adds to its vitality.

234

CRAWFORD   *Christmas.* 1938

CONCLUSION

Since there are unavoidable boundaries to any book, many worthy self-taught painters have been omitted. Some of them are well known, others are not. And there are scores yet to come to light.

A list follows of known painters whose work might very well have been included: Dr. Stan Bauch, Joseph Gatto, Lillie Sobel, Bertha Trabich, Charles Norman, Ruth Livingston, all of New York; Dr. Frederick M. Margaretten, A. Mandel, Brooklyn; John Enos, Provincetown; Patrick Taccard, Liberty, N. Y.; Laura Steig, Jersey City; Alex Fletcher, Greensburg, Pa.; Laura Elliott Weller, Rockwood, Pa.; Ara, Los Angeles; Père Hiler, San Francisco; Pearl Laskoski, Des Moines; and the gifted painter recommended by Daniel Catton Rich, S. S. Bronesky of Chicago, who prefers to have his work remain unknown. Several interesting painters are also to be found in the WPA Adult Art Classes in New York, where they are encouraged rather than taught to paint.

Painters of outstanding merit like Leon Hartl, Arnold Friedman, Vincent Canadé, Sarah Berman and Mark Baum, all of New York; Gus Mager, Newark; T. A. Hoyer, Chicago, have developed knowing styles that remove them from the category as represented in the book.

America in all its vastness, with much of the field still untouched, must in the future yield many self-taught artists. Because of their natural reticence, it is often difficult to find them, but there is no doubt that a diligent research, and a cognizance on the part of the self-taught painter that there may exist an appreciation of his work, will bring to light other important talents.